SOCIAL ISSUES, JUSTICE AND STATUS

INTERSECTIONALITY

CONCEPTS, PERSPECTIVES AND CHALLENGES

SOCIAL ISSUES, JUSTICE AND STATUS

Additional books and e-books in this series can be found
on Nova's website under the Series tab.

SOCIAL ISSUES, JUSTICE AND STATUS

INTERSECTIONALITY

CONCEPTS, PERSPECTIVES AND CHALLENGES

THOMAS MOELLER
EDITOR

Copyright © 2020 by Nova Science Publishers, Inc.

All rights reserved. No part of this book may be reproduced, stored in a retrieval system or transmitted in any form or by any means: electronic, electrostatic, magnetic, tape, mechanical photocopying, recording or otherwise without the written permission of the Publisher.

We have partnered with Copyright Clearance Center to make it easy for you to obtain permissions to reuse content from this publication. Simply navigate to this publication's page on Nova's website and locate the "Get Permission" button below the title description. This button is linked directly to the title's permission page on copyright.com. Alternatively, you can visit copyright.com and search by title, ISBN, or ISSN.

For further questions about using the service on copyright.com, please contact:
Copyright Clearance Center
Phone: +1-(978) 750-8400   Fax: +1-(978) 750-4470   E-mail: info@copyright.com.

NOTICE TO THE READER

The Publisher has taken reasonable care in the preparation of this book, but makes no expressed or implied warranty of any kind and assumes no responsibility for any errors or omissions. No liability is assumed for incidental or consequential damages in connection with or arising out of information contained in this book. The Publisher shall not be liable for any special, consequential, or exemplary damages resulting, in whole or in part, from the readers' use of, or reliance upon, this material. Any parts of this book based on government reports are so indicated and copyright is claimed for those parts to the extent applicable to compilations of such works.

Independent verification should be sought for any data, advice or recommendations contained in this book. In addition, no responsibility is assumed by the Publisher for any injury and/or damage to persons or property arising from any methods, products, instructions, ideas or otherwise contained in this publication.

This publication is designed to provide accurate and authoritative information with regard to the subject matter covered herein. It is sold with the clear understanding that the Publisher is not engaged in rendering legal or any other professional services. If legal or any other expert assistance is required, the services of a competent person should be sought. FROM A DECLARATION OF PARTICIPANTS JOINTLY ADOPTED BY A COMMITTEE OF THE AMERICAN BAR ASSOCIATION AND A COMMITTEE OF PUBLISHERS.

Additional color graphics may be available in the e-book version of this book.

Library of Congress Cataloging-in-Publication Data

ISBN: 978-1-53617-110-5

Published by Nova Science Publishers, Inc. † New York

CONTENTS

Preface		vii
Chapter 1	"I'm Representing All Black People" A Case Study of the Intersectional Experiences of STEM Students Transferring from an HBCU to a Diverse Urban University *David M. Sparks, Kathryn Pole and Jason Denhartog*	1
Chapter 2	I'm Not Going to Choose a Side Hermana: Adding Voices of Bisexual Latinx Women to an Intersectional Minority Stress Model *Dumayi Maria Gutierrez*	27
Chapter 3	Adding Interactions in Order to Model Intersectionality: An Empirical Study on Self-Perceived Health Status in Argentina *Matías S. Ballesteros and Mercedes Krause*	55
Bibliography		81
Index		133
Related Nova Publications		141

PREFACE

Intersectionality: Concepts, Perspectives and Challenges first presents a study wherein two students, one male and one female, were interviewed about their transition from a historically black college and university undergraduate program to a predominantly white institution for their graduate studies in biochemistry. The students had similar undergraduate experiences and both shared feelings of isolation, the drawbacks of academic rigor in graduate STEM programs, and the need to represent both themselves and their race.

Next, the authors explore narrative responses of bisexual Latinx women and, through an intersectionality lens, adapted the minority stress model to include their experiences. This study further supports the need for intersectional minority stress research and a necessary focus on sexually marginalized bisexual Latinx women.

The closing chapter summarizes the way in which intersectionality has been at the center of both feminist debates and the theory of gender. In the United States, Canada and Europe, it has achieved a hegemonic status strengthened by its multiple possible applications.

Chapter 1 - Using face-to-face semi-structured interviews and a focus group, two students, one male and one female, were interviewed about their transition from a Historically Black College and University (HBCU) undergraduate program to a Predominantly White Institution (PWI) for their graduate studies in Biochemistry. The students had similar undergraduate experiences and both shared feelings of isolation, the drawbacks of academic rigor in graduate STEM programs, and the need to represent both themselves and their race. The conversations also explored their identities as an African-American student and as a student of STEM, their gender expectations, and their relationships with other students of color. The paper ends with a discussion of the need for analyzing the identity development of African-American university students, the importance of representation that matches a student's intersectional identity, and recommendations for seemingly diverse graduate programs to assist in the transition experiences of STEM students from HBCU learning environments.

Chapter 2 - Recent research has begun to focus on intersectionality of sexually marginalized Latinx populations, highlighting uniqueness of cultural factors and navigating multiple marginalized identities. However, most research has been conducted with lesbian and gay Latinx individuals, leaving little attention to intersectional bisexual Latinx experiences. The present study explored narrative responses of bisexual Latinx women and, through an intersectionality lens, adapted the Minority Stress Model to include their experiences. Thematic analysis was used to analyze semi-structured interviews of 10 bisexual Latinx women. Four major themes emerged from analysis: (a) Proximal Stress: Concealment Among Family; (b) Distal Stress: Gender Discrimination; (c) Distal Stress: Religiosity, and (d) Ameliorative Factor: Religious Identity. Each theme resulted in subthemes. Discussion emphasized the exclusive descriptions of participants, multiple identity integration, and their relation to the Minority Stress Model. This study further supports the need for intersectional minority stress research and a necessary focus on sexually marginalized bisexual Latinx women.

Chapter 3 - In recent decades, intersectionality has been at the center of both feminist debates and the theory of gender. In the United States, Canada and Europe, it has achieved a hegemonic status, strengthened by its multiple possible applications, precisely because it does not meet the necessary requirements to become a theory or conception with defined contours.

Intersectionality was mainly incorporated in qualitative studies, favoring methodologies that were deemed to be best suited to address the complexity which lies within (e.g., ethnography, deconstruction, genealogy, ethnomethodology and case studies). In the field of population health research in particular, new approaches to model intersectionality in quantitative studies are still emerging. One way of making progress in multivariate analysis has been to calculate logistic regressions models separately for men and for women. Other authors work with additive models from multiple linear regressions, where different "levels of intersectionality" are included in different steps of the regression. Another possible approach, when applying multiplicative models, is the inclusion of interaction terms in conventional regression models.

This chapter aims at contributing to these theoretical-methodological discussions about intersectionality throughout an empirical analysis of health inequalities in Argentina. More specifically, the authors use one of the many multiplicative statistical models to analyze the self-perceived health status of the population aged 18 and older, living in urban areas of Argentina. The authors address the effect of different sociodemographic and geographical variables on self-perceived health status, and then they add interactions within the regression: between gender and educational level, between gender and the income quintile and between gender and the age group.

The authors work with the data of the National Survey of Risk Factors (ENFR for Encuesta Nacional de Factores de Riesgo in Spanish, 2013), provided jointly by the National Institute of Statistics and Censuses (INDEC) and the National Ministry of Health in Argentina (MSAL). This survey was carried out based on a probabilistic design (by conglomerates and stratified), throughout four stages (department, area, housing and household member). The final database is made up of 32,365 cases nationwide.

In: Intersectionality
Editor: Thomas Moeller

ISBN: 978-1-53617-110-5
© 2020 Nova Science Publishers, Inc.

Chapter 1

"I'M REPRESENTING ALL BLACK PEOPLE" A CASE STUDY OF THE INTERSECTIONAL EXPERIENCES OF STEM STUDENTS TRANSFERRING FROM AN HBCU TO A DIVERSE URBAN UNIVERSITY

David M. Sparks[1],*, Kathryn Pole[1] and Jason Denhartog[2]
[1]Department of Curriculum and Instruction,
University of Texas at Arlington, Arlington, Texas, US
[2]University of Texas at Arlington, Arlington, Texas

ABSTRACT

Using face-to-face semi-structured interviews and a focus group, two students, one male and one female, were interviewed about their transition from a Historically Black College and University (HBCU) undergraduate program to a Predominantly White Institution (PWI) for their graduate studies in Biochemistry. The students had similar undergraduate experiences and both shared feelings of isolation, the drawbacks of academic rigor in graduate STEM programs, and the need to represent both

---

* Corresponding author: David M. Sparks, Ed. D., University of Texas at Arlington, Arlington, Texas, US, E-mail: david.sparks@uta.edu.

themselves and their race. The conversations also explored their identities as an African-American student and as a student of STEM, their gender expectations, and their relationships with other students of color. The paper ends with a discussion of the need for analyzing the identity development of African-American university students, the importance of representation that matches a student's intersectional identity, and recommendations for seemingly diverse graduate programs to assist in the transition experiences of STEM students from HBCU learning environments.

Keywords: STEM, intersectionality, intersectional adaptation theory, graduate school, HBCU

INTRODUCTION

For African-American students in Science, Technology, Engineering, and Mathematics (STEM) programs, transferring from a Historically Black Colleges and Universities (HBCU) into a Predominantly White University (PWI) can be accompanied by questions about representation, academic rigor, self-efficacy, and isolation. These can occur because their undergraduate institutions were perceived as having a lack of rigor, longing for the personal interactions from their undergraduate experience, or from being one of a small number of students who *look like them* in their college courses (McClain, 2014). This case study follows two students (one male and one female) who graduated from an HBCU and enrolled in a Master's Degree program in Biochemistry at a large, diverse, urban university. Although the university is a Predominantly White Institution (PWI), it is also a Minority Serving Institution (MSI) and a Hispanic Serving Institution (HSI). The university student body is composed of approximately 14% Black, 26% Latino, .3% Native American, 38% White, 12% Asian, and 9.7% International and other (College Results Online, 2018), and has been ranked near the top of public universities for undergraduate diversity (US News & World Report, 2018).

However, within the Department of Chemistry and Biochemistry, there is a general lack of diversity for both faculty and graduate students, specifically in Latino and African-American populations. Out of 20 faculty members, there is only one African-American (a female) and one Latino (a male). Within the graduate student population of 72, there are two African-American students (one male and one female), and 3 Latino students (two female and one male). Although the department is diverse in terms of White and international student presence, it lacks equal representation of African-American and Latino students in both faculty and student populations. The experiences of the two students will be analyzed to better understand the unique challenges they faced when transferring to their graduate program of study. A qualitative methodological approach has been used to highlight the lived experiences of the two African-American students (Winkle-Wagner & McCoy, 2018) as they navigate their graduate-level STEM environment.

Students build their identities as a student of STEM as they enter college and decide on a major (Aschbacher, Li, & Roth, 2010). Ethnic identities may be equally important for members of underrepresented groups (Tate & Linn, 2009; Zirkel, 2002; Settles, 2006), and in particular for African-American students (Brown, Mangram, Sun, Cross, and Raab, 2017; Armstrong & Jovanovic, 2016; McClain, 2014). Over the course of their undergraduate preparation at HBCUs, African-American students are immersed in communities of like-minded Africans and African-Americans who are peers, faculty, and mentors. As students leave these *monocultures* and enroll in graduate school (or enter the workforce), they begin again the process of forming communities of practice in their new environments. Faced with these new *cultural domains*, students must pick and choose the connections they feel are necessary to be successful, which may include isolating themselves from new experiences or choosing to withdraw themselves from participate in home and community activities (Wenger, 1998).

As a student begins to become a part of their new community, an internal struggle develops between the student's (a) need to feel a part of the community and (b) possession of control over their decision of whether or not to interact with the dominant group. This precarious connection to the community is always under negotiation within the individual and subject to change based on their current social situation. As well, students sometimes act as brokers between their different communities of practice, or between their macroculture (home and family) and their microculture (STEM major), to help navigate the intricacies of the STEM domain (Mark, 2017). For African American students, they may also need mentors and role models that represent their unique intersectional identities, i.e., African-American male or African-American female (Sparks, 2018).

Wenger (1998) maintains that identity formation always occurs in social settings and around other students and significant adult peers. While in their communities of practice, students make friends, form connections with professors and advisors, and bond in social organizations outside of school such as fraternities and sororities (Hendricks, 1996). Students also desire not only to be a part of that community, but to also have a hand in shaping the norms of the community by their presence. Thus, the students need to feel the power to belong and also the power to be an agent of change (Wenger, 1998). This negotiating of identity in the field of STEM may cause the student to break ties with other communities in order to be accepted as a part of the new community. In this new community, a transformation occurs as they learn how to navigate, adjust, and be successful as a student and future STEM professional. It is essential to understand that identity formation and renewal never ceases throughout the human lifespan as people move in and out of work and social communities. As Wenger (1998) says, "We need to think about education not merely in terms of an initial period of socialization into a culture, but more fundamentally in terms of rhythms by which communities and individuals continually renew themselves" (p. 263).

Insights into how students navigate their communities of practice can be derived from the field of anthropology and the concept of *acculturation*. Redfield, Linton, and Herskovits (1936) originally defined acculturation as a "phenomena which results when groups of individuals having different cultures come into continuous firsthand contact with subsequent changes in the original culture patterns of either or both groups" (p. 149). It is also evident that there is likely to be conflict when two cultures occupy the same social space (Trimble, 2003). Berry (1980) maintained that acculturation involves not only the group (social acculturation) but also the individual (psychological acculturation). Berry (1980) also believed in *situational acculturation*. This means the way students adapt to the culture depends on whether they are in a familiar setting with family and/or friends (macroculture) or at their work/educational institution (microculture).

From their earliest beginnings in the post-Civil War reconstruction era, HBCUs have been leaders in the education of African-Americans. Leading up to the end of legalized segregation in the 1950s and 1960s, HBCUs were the only choice for a college education for approximately 80% of African-American college students (Lundy-Wagner, 2013). In the last few decades, HBCUs have graduated a significant number of African-Americans in STEM-related fields, including 22% of the degrees conferred to African-Americans in science and engineering bachelor's degrees in 2006 (NSF, 2010). Between 2003 and 2007, seven of the top ten producers of STEM degrees for African-American students were from HBCUs (NSF, 2009). HBCUs strive to provide a comfortable atmosphere in which the students can learn and grow together, connect with students and mentors of the same race, establish close family-like ties to a community of scholars, instill a sense of pride, confidence, and determination (Joseph, 2012; Taylor & Olswang, 1997), and help students adapt to college life (Joseph, 2013). Despite these many benefits and features of an HBCU education, PWIs and their faculty may perceive the students' HBCU education to be insufficient or sub-par (Joseph, 2013). This bias could contribute to a nearly 50% attrition rate amongst African-American students in the first two years of graduate school (Herzig, 2004; Bethea, 2005).

Students must navigate the change in atmosphere and culture from an HBCU to a PWI, including personalities, mentor relationships, and departmental norms (Joseph, 2012). In contrast to the welcoming atmosphere HBCUs offer, the transition to graduate school for many African-American STEM students can only be described as *chilly*. African-American students who have remediation needs, work under conditions of isolation, and lack commitment to complete the program will have additional issues with adjustment (Hamilton, 2001). Further, PWIs can be places of indifference where students may be expected to work exclusively within their departments, independently, and with sparse advice and mentoring (Morelle, 1996). Although the atmosphere may not be overtly hostile, PWI graduate STEM programs may inadvertently cause students to feel they are on their own and that success or failure are completely on their shoulders (Joseph, 2012). Many African-American students moving from an HBCU to a new PWI university environment experience *culture shock*, whereas most of their White or international graduate school classmates grew accustomed to the PWI environment in their undergraduate experience.

The purposes of this study are to better understand the experiences of African-American students, including (1) the unique challenges they face when transferring from a HBCU to a PWI for graduate STEM education; (2) how they adjust to different kinds of diversity (including their interactions with African international students); and (3) the importance of their interactions and relationships with friends, faculty, mentors, and role models who match their intersectional identity.

METHODS

Design

A case study design (Creswell, 2007) helped provide an understanding of the students' transition from a small, historically Black college to a large, urban, diverse university. As Creswell (2007) argues, there is not a set number of cases required for a multiple case study. Using Creswell's (2007) guidelines and criteria described by Stake (2006), two graduate students were selected to provide insight into this transition. A semi-structured interview protocol was developed based on a review of literature, informed by the data collected, and analyzed by the research team (Arksey & Knight, 1999).

During the interviews, participants were asked about their transition from a small HBCU to a large urban university. The interviewer then asked further questions to clarify and expand on initial responses. For the focus group, additional questions were asked to clarify points in the face-to-face interviews. This study was approved by the university's Institutional Review Board in 2016.

Participants

This paper focuses on two graduate students, Dania and Donald (pseudonyms). Both Dania and Donald transferred from a small historically Black university, where they earned undergraduate degrees in Chemistry. At the time of the study, they were pursuing Master's degrees in Biochemistry at a large urban university in the southwestern United States. The student population at this university is predominately White, but it is very diverse in regards to Latino and international student attendance.

Both students are involved in the Louis Stokes Alliance for Minority Participation (LSAMP) Program, a scholarship program for minorities in STEM, which paid for a significant portion of their graduate school tuition and provided feedback and mentoring. Also an LSAMP student, they also receive programming in responsible conduct of research, expectations and goal setting in graduate study, accessing internal and external financial as well as social resources, proposal writing, effective teaching practices, learning to be an effective mentor, professional communication and preparation for conferences, networking, and writing their dissertation (if they choose to continue their doctoral studies).

Both Dania and Donald attended urban high schools, and even briefly met in middle school before one of them transferred to a different local high school. Donald participated in a high school program that allowed students to pursue health careers and take classes concurrently with a local junior college. Although Donald was active in sports, he received an academic scholarship from the HBCU. His interest in Chemistry blossomed at the undergraduate level, where he switched majors from Biology to Chemistry. His advisor at the HBCU, an African-American male, advised him to major in Chemistry: "He came to me and said 'If you want a challenge this will be the major for you. I think you can do it.' So I took the challenge." Donald was involved in fraternities and scholarly clubs at the HBCU. He kept odd jobs to help pay for college-related expenses and to keep his independence, but he was unsure what to do after graduation until he heard about the scholarship program.

Dania's interest in STEM-related subjects began early, when as a 7th grader she enrolled in a high school biology class and fell in love with it. She then attended a technology-focused magnet high school where she was able to study graphic design and programming languages. In college, a desire for challenge moved her to major in Chemistry: "[I said] 'I'm going to pick the hardest thing. I'm not interested in the business field or a soft science. I'm interested in *science*.' And chemistry is what I chose." Dania was an extremely active student, involved in a sorority, community service and charity work, and academic clubs. She also participated in internships each summer and gained experience as an industrial chemist.

Data Collection

The participants described their experiences transferring from a small HBCU to a larger and more diverse university through semi-structured questioning. They were also asked follow-up questions to clarify their responses and given time to reflect on and extend their thinking. Digitally recorded interviews lasting approximately one hour were conducted in a campus building, in a quiet conference room, at a center for multicultural studies at the university. The recordings were transcribed verbatim, and read and re-read by the team of authors. The first author verified the accuracy of the transcripts by listening and following along with the recorded interviews and focus group interactions, making slight adjustments to the transcripts before analysis.

Data Analysis

The interview transcripts were analyzed using thematic analysis to organize, describe, and identify patterns, and helped the researchers interpret the interview data (Braun & Clarke, 2006). This thematic analysis was grounded in the belief that as the participants talked, they were making sense of their experiences and the social context of those experiences. A theoretical approach to analysis allows a description of the data in light of the specific interview questions, which were informed by the theoretical research base (Patton, 1980). Coding and analysis were conducted with hand coding techniques and the analytical software NVivo.

RESULTS

The interviews and focus group discussions demonstrate an interesting dynamic that shows itself in the way students speak about representation. The students discuss the same graduate advisor that they are both assigned. While the advisor matches Dania's identity in two specific attributes (African-American and female), she does not *specifically* match Donald's identity (African-American and male). Although he speaks highly of the advisor, it is possible that he is lacking the connection of a mentor that matches his identity specifically as an African-American male. We also see that both students recognize the differences they have with African international students, as well as the struggles they face trying to understand the variations of diversity inherent in STEM programs at this Predominantly White Institution (PWI).

Challenges, Commitment, and Purpose

Donald conveyed that his greatest challenge was a need to *represent* himself: "Personally, I feel like I'm constantly having to prove myself at every step just because of the type of university this is. That's just something that I kind of carry with me." When asked what he meant by the *kind of university*, he elaborated by saying "I always feel like I have to step it up and always remember *'you gotta do this.'* There's not room for error for me here."

Dania also discussed issues with the rigor that she experienced in her graduate-level coursework.

> I feel like I've faced a lot of mental challenges here simply because it's a little more rigorous than what I'm used to. Some days I come to school and I feel like I'm not good enough to be in my program or I feel kind of left out because I don't know as much as other people.

She said that she had never talked to anyone about these feelings, but she knows that many students have similar struggles and are trying to do their best.

Dania and Donald both discussed their struggles with the rigor of the curriculum at their new university. Donald felt the more rigorous graduate curriculum exposed some of the deficiencies he had: "You really gotta know everything. It just takes an amount of time and effort. And sometimes knowing that I need some help and knowing how to ask for it, I think that's my biggest issue." Dania agreed: "Sometimes it can be information overload if you're taking 2 or 3 courses. And when they make their tests, they ask you the very smallest detail that you probably overlooked." Dania also stated that she loved her HBCU coursework and felt that the atmosphere at HBCUs of accepting students with lower academic backgrounds and ACT scores helps those students. However, it does not push other students like her as far as they need to be, especially when preparing to transfer into a rigorous graduate STEM program.

A Different Kind of Diversity

How do students who transfer from an environment that is almost exclusively African and African-American adjust to a type of diversity that also includes a large and diverse international populations? It may relate to what a student considers *diversity*, and Dania and Donald have similar definitions. Donald sees diversity in his current university's focus on representing a wide variety of students, including global and international populations. His HBCU focuses on "Black people, people or color, and other minorities." Dania believes diversity is all about providing opportunities for many different groups.

She also believes her current university focuses more on international populations, while her HBCU focuses on providing opportunities for minorities and African-Americans. Although the goals of diversity for each type of university seems incongruent, both students said the diversity of the graduate school was beneficial, introduced them to a number of different students, and was an overall positive experience.

Discussing diversity at his present university, Donald remarked: "I guess one thing I learned about the diversity here is that I've never experienced so many cultures. I've never been able to see a group of different types of students or international students, how they interact." Donald also described the transition from the HBCU as *culture shock*:

> It *was* a culture shock coming here. I didn't grow up really in a minority setting other than when I interacted outside of school. We went to a majority Black school. I had different races at my school, but the overwhelming majority have all been African-American or Latino. And that was all the way up through college.

During the course of the interviews, the discussion came around to the differences between African international students and African-American students. Dania believed there are some major differences: "I personally feel like African-American people and African people are two totally different types of people. And they don't necessarily feel and believe the same things. And sometimes I feel like they don't like each other…you feel tension sometimes." On a positive note, she praised the African students: "I feel like they already have the motivation to follow their plans and they're willing to work hard for what they want."

Donald agreed: "I think that, for many international students, you have to be really smart or talented to leave one country and go to a whole other country for school. They're already on a higher level." Overall, both students believe there is no overt animosity between African-American students and the African international students. There is only a recognition of difference. As far as competition with African students, Donald felt he was competing against *everyone*, and African students are just one of those groups.

Race, Racism, and Representation

Both students, but more-so Donald, felt the burden of representing themselves *and* representing all African-Americans. According to Donald: "I'm one of my biggest critics. I felt like I wasn't just representing myself, I felt I was representing everybody else because I know after me they may remember that [about] all of their Black students." Speaking of *us*, he was referring to successful Black males in academia, specifically in graduate school. Even from his days at the HBCU, he was taught that he had to present himself in a different way:

> We were always taught, even prior to coming to my HBCU, I had to be better. So I just knew when it's the real world, I don't have room for mistakes. I need to dress well, look well, speak well. You need to be good because society doesn't expect this from you. It's not just, "Be the best you can be just for you." You have to be better because society already has a view of you.

When asked if she felt the pressure to perform and act certain ways as an African-American student, Dania said "Mom always told me, you always gotta do things better, say things better, dress better. You have to do everything better. And not to make you feel superior, but because other people make you feel inferior."

Donald felt from a young age that he stood out academically, and in regards to maturity, in a mostly Black environment, and this was especially evident during his time at the HBCU. This was also a time when he really felt that he grew in his racial identity by being around many Black peers, faculty, mentors, and role models. He also shared that he is currently the only Black male in most of his Master's degree classes. Although this reality did encourage him, he still had reservations.

> It encourages me, but I think it puts an added little pressure because I feel like for some people, I'm the only representation of what you see for a Black male or a Black person in general. And so in my head I feel like it's my job not only to break stereotypes. I'm supposed to be me, but I [also] feel like I'm supposed to be the best perception of me. Because I

know I'm not only representing myself, [but] I feel like I'm representing all Black people.

Questions related to identity, and how they would like to be described, brought up issues of how Dania and Donald want to both represent themselves and be represented by others. Dania believed her race would not be an important trait to bring up if she was describing herself to someone: "I am a young, aspiring chemist and biochemist. I feel like *Black* has nothing to do with it. At the end of the day, that is what I am." When asked if she had ever experienced any kind of racism or stereotyping, she had this to say:

> We'll, it's not very direct. I don't even want to call it stereotyping. No one's even said anything to me. But I know that my lab group, in our department, is the most colorful lab. That's what I've heard before. Because we have people from every country. We have Indian students and Black students. My professor is Black; the only Black woman in the department. And I don't think a lot of the white males support her. It feels like they don't really want her here.

Donald, speaking about his personal identity, said he would probably focus more on the STEM aspect than his *Blackness*.

Both students have strong opinions on why there is underrepresentation of African-American students in STEM fields. Donald felt it was primarily related to exposure: "You don't see Black scientists, you don't see too many Black engineers where I'm from. You don't see too many Black doctors. So I think if you don't see it, some kids aren't drawn to that." He also mentioned that he had an older brother with friends that were PhD students and engineers, and that really helped mentor him. But he rarely saw examples of advanced professional role models in high school who were also Black.

Dania's reasoning for the reality of fewer African-Americans in STEM went back to rigor and opportunities:

> It's hard and it's just very technical. And I don't think a lot of people really have the patience to sit down and learn things. I feel like different things affect people's will to learn. Some people may need to get jobs early to support their family, so they can't really focus on school. Whereas me, my mom told me "don't get a job in high school. You need to go to college.

You need to do these things just because in my family, no one did those things."

She also stated that it would be helpful for Black students to see Black role models in the different STEM careers and stressed the importance of serving as a mentor. In the past, she mentored students that were transferring into STEM careers at her HBCU and she is currently active in mentoring young girls in STEM with her sorority.

Gender in STEM

Both Dania and Donald had opinions about the struggles they had faced related to their gender. Dania felt like the pressures of being a woman and a graduate student are high: "I feel like there's a lot of pressure at this point to have a family. And I feel like being a graduate student and getting married and having children, it's a lot." She also stated gender norms are both society-based and gender-related. She also believed that female students are naturally drawn to more nurturing roles: "I feel like women tend to go to those kinds of fields where they're more nurturing and caring. Men choose more technical fields where they can do business or get a degree in math or science."

As far as how to attract more females into STEM careers, she believes job shadowing and taking tours of industries and labs run by women would go a long way: "Sometimes [girls] don't know how it applies to life and how it makes people feel and how it helps people. I think you just have to see the bigger picture and *then* get technical." As far the barriers her African-American female mentor faced, she felt that the professor did not get the respect she deserves from her male peers. "I just feel like they think women should be at home. You know, cooking and cleaning and taking care of babies. It's hard for [my mentor] to balance her life being a single mother, a professor, and enjoying life."

When asked about how being a male has affected his exposure to STEM, in both negative and positive ways, Donald believed Black males have their own set of struggles: "I do feel like Black males have different things that are fighting against them. Not just from a societal standpoint…both school and society. I don't think a lot of [Black students] can handle *not* seeing someone like [themselves]." Donald repeatedly went back to how African-American men are perceived in STEM, but also in a general sense of being a successful Black male. For him, representation is important to both males in STEM and all Black males in which he interacts. As far as what he felt would attract more Black males into STEM, he believes that exposure to programs and resources related to financial aid and scholarships are crucial to their success. Without those financial resources he received throughout high school and college, he would not be where he is today. Donald said he still gets excited when he sees Black males in a STEM environment: "I'm ecstatic to go to a seminar where there is a Black male speaker. I like to speak to them about some of the challenges they've faced because there's not a lot of *us*."

CONCLUSION

There are many similarities in the testimonies of these two students. Both exhibit pride and take comfort in their HBCU experiences. Both Dania and Donald tended to work and study alone without asking for help, and struggle with the academic rigor of their new university. They also both feel connected to the larger African-American community and feel it is important to give back and mentor other African-American students interested in STEM. Both feel the burden of representing themselves and also their race. This *burden of representation* was mentioned a number of times and is something that should be explored in future research. In other studies, this phenomenon in African-American students has been referred to as *Prove-Them-Wrong Syndrome* (Vega, Moore, & Miranda, 2015; Moore, Madison-Colmore, & Smith, 2003) and *intersectional adaptation theory* (Sparks, 2018). Although Dania seemed to focus only on her identity as a female, Donald focused on his identity as an *African-American male*, stating that he has felt the burden of representing Black males and, at his graduate university, the isolation of not having African-American male mentors like he had at the HBCU. Thus, Donald expressed that there is a lack of *intersectional representation* of African American males in STEM at his graduate-level university.

According to research regarding the success and graduation rates of African-American students at HBCUs (Solorzano, 1995; NSF, 2010), it is evident that HBCUs prepare their students in ways that include academic, psychological, and social development. HBCUs have also been shown to be vehicles for social capital for students of color (Brown & Davis, 2001), helping them build confidence, agency, and skills necessary for a successful adult life (Lappe & DuBois, 1997). They are also a place for African-American students to establish peer relationships and a sense of community that helps them complete their degrees in a timely manner (Fries-Britt, Younger, & Hall, 2010). However, this grounding does not guarantee success for African-American students who transfer to graduate STEM programs (Joseph, 2013). For students who transfer from HBCUs to PWIs, this transition can be a daunting experience (Joseph, 2010). The students must find a supportive advisor early in their transition. It is not always possible for the advisor to match the student's race and/or gender, but it is important to find an advisor that understands the struggles these students are facing. The lack of diversity and common community at the PWI, especially when compared with the faculty at the HBCU, can be both disheartening and disorienting (Joseph, 2007).

Identity may be a moderating factor in the success of these students. Studies have shown that students with strong identities, confidence, and self-efficacy may have a greater chance to fit in and succeed (Ervin, 2001). Additionally a strong sense of determination and cultural pride have been found to be beneficial (Taylor & Olswang, 1997; Zirkel & Johnson, 2016). The formation of relationships with students of the same race/ethnicity are extremely important because they share similar cultural values (Ellis, 2001; Herzig, 2004). Students feel worthwhile in these communities and are welcomed into a safe space where they can share their concerns (Ellis, 2001). While HBCUs do much to strengthen the ethnic and racial identity of their students, PWIs are not specifically focused to that end. This may be especially troublesome for African-American students transferring from an HBCU, where they are nurtured and their racial identity is strengthened.

The first two years of graduate school can be a stressful time of adjustment for all students, but even more for students transferring from an HBCU (Joseph, 2012). Goal commitment has been found to be important for students in building self-efficacy and confidence. Students who are not fully committed to their goals may be less likely to tolerate adversity and more likely to not finish their graduate programs (Leslie, McClure, & Oaxaca, 1998). Goal commitment also makes it easier for students to feel like they can fit into departmental norms and culture, ask for additional assistance such as tutoring if needed, and speak to their instructors and TAs. This can also lead to students conducting themselves in a business-like manner, changing their dress to accommodate the new environment, and interacting in such a way that will help them survive and thrive in graduate school (Joseph, 2012).

In the duration of the program from start to finish, a student will ideally transform from a college *student* to a *colleague* and evolve in their choices, behaviors, and beliefs about the community of STEM to which they will belong (Phinney, 2003). Students more likely to leave their graduate programs are those who are not well integrated into the social and academic aspects of their STEM departmental communities (Herzig, 2004). Universities strive to be diverse and also espouse the benefits of diversity, but many do not understand the racial and ethnic identities of African-American students nor strive to understand their needs as unique individuals (Brown, 2004) and the intersectionality of their race and gender (Sparks, 2017; 2018).

The onus for a graduate student feeling a vital part of the departmental culture should not be exclusively on the student. University STEM departments need to devise ways to make African-American students feel welcome and help them successfully integrate into this subculture, a process I call *domain acculturation*. For these students, acculturative stress can occur when individuals face problems related to their acculturation within a community (Barry, 1997). It would be beneficial for graduate programs to decrease student anxiety by helping students to adapt academically, psychologically, and socially into the new environment (Herzig, 2004). Theoretical frameworks such as *stereotype management* (McGee & Martin, 2011) and *intersectional adaptation theory* (Sparks, 2018) may help researchers understand the way students of color adapt to a STEM culture, including how all the interactions that make up their STEM acculturation differ from their majority peers.

Future research should investigate (1) how college students adapt under different conditions and in different contexts, (2) if marginalized students other than African-Americans adapt to their environment in similar ways, (3) the differences in domain acculturation of male and female students in STEM environments, and (4) whether African-American students' adaptations are more fluid because of their tendencies to be bicultural and acculturate on a daily basis (Landrine & Klonoff, 1996; Zirkel & Johnson, 2016). Although much research has been conducted on intersectionality (Bowleg, 2008; Carbado, Crenshaw, Mays, & Tomlinson, 2013; Crenshaw, 1991; Dill & Zambrana, 2009; Purdie-Vaughs & Eibach, 2008; Sparks, 2017; Walby, Armstrong, & Strid, 2012), identity (Brown, 2004; Gee, 2000), and acculturation (Berry, 1980; Joseph, 2012, 2013, 2014; Landrine & Klonoff, 1996; Phinney, 2003), more research needs to be done on the combination of these factors, specifically in STEM fields where students of color are underrepresented (Malcom & Malcom, 2011; Malone & Barbino, 2009; Settles, 2006). This includes research on how students of color adapt to their university graduate programs in an environment that is diverse according to university standards, but not as diverse in specifically attracting and retaining African-American students.

While a number of studies have looked at the adaptation of female college students (Beoku-Betts, 2004; Ferreira, 2002; Johnson-Bailey, 2004; Purdie-Vaughns, & Eibach, 2008; Schwartz, Bower, Rice, Washington, & 2003; Settles, 2006; Smith, 2016), only a few have explored the experiences of comparable male college students (Maton, Hrabowski, & Greif, 1998; Moore et al., 2003; Stinton, 2006), and few have looked at their unique experiences of African American males at HBCUs and PWIs. Despite evidence that African-American male students struggle with many aspects of academic study as compared to their female counterparts, Lundy-Wagner and Gasman (2011; 2013) found research related to African-American males in STEM to be lacking. Research has shown that females have made significant gains in STEM teaching and the biological sciences, while African-American males have decreased in both populations (Cheryan, Ziegler, & Montoya, 2016). Research focused on high ethnic identity (Phinney, 1990; Zirkel & Johnson, 2016), which could serve as a moderator to acculturative stress, would be beneficial. Research should also focus on how some students have parallel identities (racial and STEM) in both cultures (McClain, 2014) and the processes by which students of color serve as cultural brokers as they attempt to blend the two cultures (Padilla & Perez, 2003).

Students such as Dania and Donald transfer from an academically and culturally supportive environment where their growth and maturity is observed by numerous people of similar representation. In the HBCU environment, they share a cultural identity with the group, and, as such, feel safe. In this environment, personal identity questions may largely recede into the background. In the PWI STEM environment, where few people share overlaps of their cultural identity, personal identity questions can loom large, and consume precious time, emotion, and energy. As described by *intersectional adaptation theory* (Sparks, 2018), it is possible that some students of color thrive in the presence of peers, advisors, professors, and mentors that match their intersectional identities in terms of race, ethnicity, sex, and academic or professional domain.

Whatever institutional improvements have been made to help African-American students be successful in their graduate programs, the stark reality is that they are still an underrepresented group. As an underrepresented group, they may continue to look for individuals that share their racial and ethnic characteristics within these programs. Although growing the African-American population by only a few students seems inconsequential, it could have a lasting effect on African-American students trying to build a community within the STEM culture (Joseph, 2013). Bridge programs between HBCUs and PWIs must stress the need for community building, leveraging social capitol for success, and seeking ways to help these students adapt to a new and *differently* diverse culture with students from all over the world (Stolle-McAllister, K. 2011). If the notion of students ascribing value to intersectional connections has merit, then colleges and universities must focus not only on diversity in general, but on *compositional diversity* in particular (Winkle-Wagner & McCoy, 2018). These and other strategies, interventions, and encouragements would go a long way in producing a critical mass of confident African-American STEM professionals.

REFERENCES

Armstrong, M. A. & Jovanovic, J. (2017). The intersectional matrix: Rethinking institutional change for URM women in STEM. *Journal of Diversity in Higher Education*, *10*(3), 216-231. doi: 10.1037/dhe0000021.

Arksey, H. & Knight, P. (1999). *Interviewing for Social Scientists*. Thousand Oaks, CA: Sage.

Aschbacher, P. R., Li, E. & Roth, E. J. (2010). Is science me? High school students' identities, participation, and aspirations in Science, Engineering, and Medicine. *Journal of Research in Science Teaching*, *47*(5), 564-582. doi: 10.1002/tea.20353.

Bethea, G. (2005). *Graduate school kicks off new PhD. Retention and attrition efforts with luncheon and charge from Provost Richard English*. Washington, D.C.: Howard University.

Beoku-Betts, J. (2004). African women pursuing graduate studies in the science: Racism, gender bias, and third world marginality. *NWSA Journal*, *16*(1), 20.

Berry, J. W. (1980). Acculturation as varieties of adaptation. In A. Padilla (Ed.), *Acculturation: Theory, models and some new findings* (pp. 9-25). Boulder, CO: Westview.

Bowleg, L. (2008). When Black + lesbian + women ≠ Black lesbian woman: The methodological challenges of qualitative and quantitative intersectionality research. *Sex Roles*, *59*, 312-325.

Braun, V. and Clarke, V. (2006). Using thematic analysis in psychology. *Qualitative Research in Psychology 3*, 77-101. doi:10/1191/1478088706qp063oa.

Brown, B. A., Mangram, C., Sun, K., Cross, K., Raaab, E. (2017). Representing racial identity: Identity, race, and the construction of the African American STEM students. *Urban Education, 52*(2), 170-206. doi: 10.1177/0042085916661385.

Brown, L. I. (2004). Diversity: The challenge for higher education. *Race Ethnicity and Education, 7*(1), 21-34. doi: 10.1080/1361332042000187289.

Brown, M. C., II, & Davis, J. E. (2001). The historically black college as social contract, social capital, and social equalizer. *Peabody Journal of Education, 76*(1), 31-49.

Campus ethnic diversity. (2018, March 19). *US News & World Report*. Retrieved from https://www.usnews.com/best-colleges/rankings/national-universities/campus-ethnic-diversity.

Carbado, D. W., Crenshaw, K. W., Mays, V. M. & Tomlinson, B. (2013). Intersectionality: Mapping the movements of a theory. *Du Bois Review: Social Science Research on Race, 10*(2), 303-312.

Cheryan, S., Ziegler, S. A. & Montoya, A. K. (2017). Why are some STEM fields more gender balanced than others? *Psychological Bulletin, 143*(1), 1-35. doi:10.1037/bu10000052.

College Results Online (2016). The Education Trust. Retrieved from http://www.collegeresults.org/collegeprofile.aspx?institutionid=228769.

Crenshaw, K. W. (1991). Mapping the margins: Intersectionality, identity politics, and violence against women of color. *Stanford Law Review, 43*(6), 1241–1299.

Creswell, J. (2007). *Qualitative inquiry and research design: Choosing among five approaches (2nd ed.)* Thousand Oaks, CA: Sage.

Dill, B. T. & Zambrana, R. E. (2009). *Emerging intersections: Race, class, and gender in theory, policy, and practice.* New Brunswick, NJ: Rutgers University Press.

Ellis, E. (2001). The impact of race and gender on graduate school socialization, satisfaction with doctoral study, and commitment to degree completion. *The Western Journal of Black Studies, 25*(1), 30-45.

Ervin, K. S. (2001). Multiculturalism, diversity, and African American college students. *Journal of Black Studies, 31*(6), 764 - 776.

Ferreira, M. (2002). The research lab: A chilly place for graduate women. *Journal of Women and Minorities in Science and Engineering, 8*(1), 85-98.

Fries-Britt, S., Younger, T., & Hall, W. (2010). Lessons from high-achieving students of color in physics. In S. R. Harper & C. B. Newman (Eds.), *New Directions for Institutional Research: No. 148. Students of color in STEM* (pp. 75–83). San Francisco, CA: Jossey-Bass.

Gee, J. P. (2000). Identity as an analytic lens for research in education. *Review of Research in Education, 25*, 99-125.

Hamilton, K. (2001). Doctoral dilemma. *Black Issues in Higher Education, 18*(11), 34-37.

Hendricks, M. L. (1996). *Racial identity development of African American male fraternity members and nonmembers at historically black colleges and universities and predominantly white campuses* (Doctoral dissertation). Available from ProQuest Dissertations and Theses database. (UMI No. 9724616).

Herzig, A. H. (2004). Becoming mathematics: Women and students of color choosing and leaving doctoral mathematics. *Review of Educational Research, 74*(2), 171 - 214.

Ibarra, R. (2001). *Beyond affirmative action: Reframing the context of higher education*. Madison, WI: University of Wisconsin Press.

Johnson-Bailey, J. (2004). Hitting and climbing the proverbial wall: Participation and retention issues for Black graduate women. *Race Ethnicity and Education, 7*(4), 331-349. doi: 10.1080/1361332042000303360.

Joseph, J. (2007). *The experiences of African American graduate students: A cultural transition* (Unpublished dissertation). University of Southern California, Los Angeles.

Joseph, J. (2012). From one culture to another: Year one and two of graduate school for African-American women in the STEM fields. *International Journal of Doctoral Studies, 7,* 125-142.

Joseph, J. (2013). The impact of Historically Black Colleges and Universities on doctoral students. *New Directions for Higher Education, 163,* 67-76.

Joseph, J. (2014). Acculturation, not socialization, for African-American females in the STEM fields. *Sociological Research Online, 19*(2), 1-8. Retrieved from http://www.socresonline.org.uk/19/2/8.html.

Landrine, H. & Klonoff, E. A. (1996). *African American acculturation: deconstructing race and reviving culture.* Thousand Oaks, CA: Sage Publications.

Lappe, F. M. & DuBois, P. M. (1997). Building social capital without looking backward. *National Civic Review, 86*(2), 119–128.

Leslie, L. L., McClure, G. T. & Oaxaca, R. L. (1998). Women and minorities in science and engineering: A life sequence analysis. *Journal of Higher Education, 69,* 239-276.

Lundy-Wagner, V. C. (2013). Is it really a man's world? Black men in the science, technology, engineering, and mathematics at Historically Black Colleges and Universities. *The Journal of Negro Education, 82*(2), 157-168.

Maton, K. I., Hrabowski, F. A., III, & Greif, G. L. (1998). Preparing the way: A qualitative study of high-achieving African American males and the role of the family. *American Journal of Community Psychology, 26,* 639-668.

Malone, K. & Barbino, G. (2009). Narrations of race in STEM research settings: Identity formation and its discontents. *Science Education, 93*(3), 485-510.

Malcom, L. E. & Malcom, S. M. (2011). The double bind: The next generation. *Harvard Educational Review, 81*(2), 162-171. doi: 10.17763/haer.81.2.a84201x508406327.

Mark, S. L. (2017). A bit of both science and economics: a non-traditional STEM identity narrative. *Cultural Studies of Science Education.*

Published online 04 October 2017 https://doi.org/10.1007/s11422-017-9832-2.

McClain, O. L. (2014). Negotiating identity: A look at the educational experiences of Black undergraduates in STEM disciplines. *Peabody Journal of Education, 89*(3), 380-392. doi: 10.1080/0161956X.2014.913451.

McGee, E. O. & Martin, D. B. (2011). "You would not believe what I have to go through to prove my intellectual value!" Stereotype management among academically successful black mathematics and engineering students. *American Educational Research Journal, 48*(6), 1347-1389. doi: 10.3102/0002831211423972.

Moore, J. L., Madison-Colmore, O. & Smith, D. M. (2003). The prove-them-wrong syndrome: Voices from unheard African American males in engineering disciplines. *The Journal of Men's Studies, 12*, 61-73. doi:10.3149/jms.1201.61.

Morelle, V. (1996). Computer culture deflects women and minorities. *Science, 271*(5257), 2.

National Science Foundation. (2009). *Top baccalaureate institutions of black S &E doctorate recipients: 2003-07. Women, minorities, and persons with disabilities in science and engineering.* Washington, DC: National Science Foundation.

National Science Foundation. (2010). 2010 *Science and engineering degrees, by race/ethnicity of recipients: 1997–2006.* (Tables NSF 10-300). Arlington, VA. Retrieved from http://www.nsf.gov/statistics/nsf10300/.

Padilla, A. & Perez, W. (2003). Acculturation, social identity, and social cognition: A new perspective. *Hispanic Journal of Behavioral Sciences, 25*(1), 35-55. doi://dx.doi.org/10.1177/0739986303251694.

Patton, M. Q. (1980). *Qualitative evaluation and research methods*, 2nd ed. Beverly Hills, CA: Sage.

Phinney, J. (1990). Ethnic identity in adolescents and adults: Review of research. *Psychological Bulletin, 108*(3), 499-514. doi://dx.doi.org/10.1037/0033-2909.108.3.499.

Phinney, J. (2003). Ethnic identity and acculturation. In K. Chun, P. Organista, & G. Marin (Eds.), *Acculturation* (pp. 63-81). Washington DC: American Psychological Association.

Purdie-Vaughns, V., & Eibach, R. P. (2008). Intersectional invisibility: The distinctive advantages and disadvantages of multiple subordinate-group identities. *Sex Roles, 59*(5–6), 377–91.

Redfield, R., Linton, R. & Herskovits, M. (1936). A Memorandum for the Study of Acculturation. *Man, 35*, 145 - 148.

Schwartz, R. A., Bower, B. L., Rice, D. C. & Washington, C. M. (2003). Ain't I a woman, too? Tracing the experiences of African American women in graduate school. *Journal of Negro Education, 72*(3), 252 - 268.

Settles, I. (2006). Use of an intersectional framework to understand Black women's racial and gender identities. *Sex Roles, 54*, 589-601. doi:10.1007/s11199-006-9029-8.

Smith, D. J. (2016). Operating in the middle: The experiences of African American female transfer students in STEM degree programs at HBCUs. *Community College Journal of Research and Practice, 40*(12), 1025-1039. doi: 10.1080/10668926.2016.1206841.

Solórzano, D. (1995). The doctorate production and baccalaureate origins of African Americans in the sciences and engineering. *Journal of Negro Education, 64*(1), 15–32.

Stake, R. E. (2006) *Multiple case study analysis*. New York, NY: The Guilford Press.

Stinton, D. W. (2006). African American male adolescents, schooling (and mathematics): Deficiency, rejection, and achievement. *Review of Educational Research, 76*, 477-506.

Sparks, D. (2017). Navigating STEM-worlds: Applying a lens of intersectionality to the career identity development of underrepresented female students of color. *Journal for Multicultural Education, 11*(3), 162-175, doi: 10.1108/JME-12-2015-0049.

Sparks, D. (2018). The process of becoming: Identity development of African-American female science and mathematics pre-service teachers.

Journal of Science Teacher Education, 29(3), 243-261. doi: 10.1080/1046560X.2018.1436359.

Stolle-McAllister, K. (2011, Fall). The case for summer bridge: Building social and cultural capital for talented Black STEM students. *Science Educator, 20*(2), 12-22.

Tate, E. & Linn, M. (2005). How does identity shape the experiences of women of color engineering students? *Journal of Science Education and Technology, 14*(5), 483-493.

Taylor, E. & Olswang, S. (1997). Crossing the color line: African Americans and predominantly white universities. *College Student Journal, 31*(1), 11-18.

Trimble, J. E. (2003). Introduction: Social change and acculturation. In K. Chun, P. Organista, & G. Marin (Eds.), *Acculturation* (pp. 3-13). Washington DC: American Psychological Association.

Vega, D., Moore III, J. L. & Miranda, A. H. (2015). "I'm Going to Prove You Wrong" Responses to perceived discrimination among African American youth. *Journal for Multicultural Education, 9*(4), 210-224. doi: 10.1108/JME-11-2014-0037.

Walby, S., Armstrong, J. & Strid, S. (2012) Intersectionality: Multiple inequalities in social theory. *Sociology, 46*(2), 224–240. doi: 10.1177/0038038511416164.

Wenger, E. (1998). *Communities of practice: Learning, meaning, and identity*. New York: Cambridge University Press.

Winkle-Wagner, R. & McCoy, D. L. (2018). Feeling like an "alien" or "family"? Comparing students and faculty experiences of diversity in STEM disciplines at a PWI and an HBCU. *Race, Ethnicity, and Education, 21*(5), 593-606. doi: 10.1080/13613324.2016.1248835.

Zirkel, S. (2002). Is there a place for me? Role models and academic identity among white students and students of color. *Teachers College Record, 104*(2), 357 – 376.

Zirkel, S. & Johnson, T. (2016). Mirror, mirror on the wall: A critical examination of the conceptualization of the study of Black racial identity in education. *Educational Researcher, 45*(5), 301-311. doi: 10.3102/0013189X16656938.

In: Intersectionality
Editor: Thomas Moeller

ISBN: 978-1-53617-110-5
© 2020 Nova Science Publishers, Inc.

Chapter 2

I'M NOT GOING TO CHOOSE A SIDE HERMANA: ADDING VOICES OF BISEXUAL LATINX WOMEN TO AN INTERSECTIONAL MINORITY STRESS MODEL

Dumayi Maria Gutierrez[*]
Couple and Family Therapy,
University of Iowa, Iowa City, IA, US

ABSTRACT

Recent research has begun to focus on intersectionality of sexually marginalized Latinx populations, highlighting uniqueness of cultural factors and navigating multiple marginalized identities. However, most research has been conducted with lesbian and gay Latinx individuals, leaving little attention to intersectional bisexual Latinx experiences. The present study explored narrative responses of bisexual Latinx women and, through an intersectionality lens, adapted the Minority Stress Model to include their experiences. Thematic analysis was used to analyze semi-structured interviews of 10 bisexual Latinx women. Four major themes emerged from analysis: (a) Proximal Stress: Concealment Among Family;

---

[*] Corresponding Email: Dumayi-gutierrez@uiowa.edu.

(b) Distal Stress: Gender Discrimination; (c) Distal Stress: Religiosity, and (d) Ameliorative Factor: Religious Identity. Each theme resulted in subthemes. Discussion emphasized the exclusive descriptions of participants, multiple identity integration, and their relation to the Minority Stress Model. This study further supports the need for intersectional minority stress research and a necessary focus on sexually marginalized bisexual Latinx women.

Keywords: intersectionality, minority stress, bisexual, Latinx, religiosity, familism, gender

INTRODUCTION

Experiences of sexually marginalized Latinxs have been central to evolving intersectional multicultural research, yet bisexual narratives have been excluded (Acosta, 2010; Dutwin, 2012; Ryan, Russell, Huebner, Diaz & Sanchez, 2010; Herek & Rivera, 2006). Unfortunately, this trend is not restricted to academic research but is constant in bisexual individuals lives. Bisexual individuals experience exclusion from heterosexual, marginalized sexual and gender communities and society at large (McLean, 2008). Exclusion leads to bisexual women experiencing higher negative mental health outcomes such as anxiety, mood disorders, depression and suicide attempts (Bostwick, Boyd, Hughes & McCabe, 2010; Cochran, Mays, Alegria, Ortega & Takeuchi, 2007). Bisexual Latinx women may experience these outcomes twofold from repeating cycles of gender, ethnicity and sexuality oppression. (Davis, 2008; Sue & Sue, 2013). Using an intersectionality lens, the purpose of this qualitative study was to explore bisexual Latinx women's narratives through cultural factors (religiosity, familism and gender) and adapt them into the minority stress model. Ultimately, bringing voices of marginalized bisexual Latinas to the forefront of intersectional research.

Intersectionality

A leading figure in intersectionality work, Kimberely Crenshaw, describes how intersectionality is centered on the connections between identities and how individuals navigate these connections with oppression from societal power (Crenshaw 1991; Cho, Crenshaw, & McCall, 2013). Applying Crenshaw's work to specifically understand women with multiple marginalized identities and identity interaction is crucial. Literature on Latinx culture is saturated with one dimensional frameworks, lacking multidimensionality of experiences (Adames, Chavez-Dueñas, Sharma & La Roche, 2018). Bisexual Latinx women are a community that fall within one dimensional frameworks and grouping into lesbian identities, completely leaving out the bi experience (Barker, Yockney, Richards, Jones, Bowes-Catton & Plowman, 2012). This study shifts from one dimensional to multidimensionality and integration of cultural factors.

Minority Stress

The minority stress model discusses unique experiences by sexually marginalized individuals. The model is based on intergroup relations theory, emphasizing the importance of social environment interaction and conflicts of marginalized/dominate societal norms (Meyer, 2003). Minority stressors include distal stress (objective stress that is influenced by social relationships such as discrimination and prejudice), proximal stress (subjective intrapersonal stress such as internalized heterosexism, expectations of rejection and concealment), ameliorating factors (coping resources and social support), and mental health outcomes (Meyer, 2003). This model has been widely used in sexually marginalized research including ethnicity (Balsam, Molina, Beadnell, Simoni & Walters, 2011; Lehavot & Simoni, 2011), transgender and gender non-conforming community (Hendricks & Testa, 2012), relationship influence (Balsam & Szymanski, 2005; Frost & Meyer, 2009), and HIV-related stigma (Hamilton & Mahalik, 2009; Hatzenbuehler, Nolen-Hoeksema & Erickson, 2008;

Logie, Newman, Chakrapani & Shunmugam, 2012). However, this model has lacked in incorporating unique experiences and cultural factors. Specifically, factors from bisexual Latinx women are completely absent from the model and warrants immediate integration.

Latinx Cultural Factors

Religiosity

Religiosity and its practices are core to Latinx culture. Religious beliefs, particularly Roman Catholicism, has been practiced in Latinx communities dating back to 1500's colonial slaved trades to ensure the continuation of tradition and culture (Akerlund & Cheung, 2000; Arana, 2001). Practices have continued to be a foundation to Latinx culture by including religious participation in churches, sanctity of marriage and family value (Espinosa, 2008).

Uniquely, adherence to traditional religiosity in Latinx families has contributed to emotional and social support (Skinner, Correa, Skinner & Bailey, 2001), and access to alternative healing resources from language or economic barriers (Ransford, Carrillo & Rivera, 2010). Even from an early childhood, religion provides values and principles to guide actions, develop a sense of purpose, self-identity, and strength (García, Gray-Stanley & Ramirez-Valles, 2008). Thus, portraying how significant religiosity is throughout a lifetime for this community.

Religiosity and Sexual Identity in Latinx Culture

Religiosity in Latinx culture has been a source of tension for Latinx with sexually marginalized identities (García, Gray-Stanley & Ramirez-Valles, 2008). The relationship between value of religiosity in Latinx culture and rejection is a unique stressor encountered by Latinx individuals with integrative identities. Latinx from highly religious families may experience rejection because of their sexual orientation (Acosta, 2010; Ryan, Huebner, Diaz & Sanchez, 2009).

Sexually marginalized Latinx individuals do not just experience rejection from their family, but experiences rejection from their churches and community (García et al., 2008). It is important to note here that not all religions affiliations are non-affirming, however, those that do cast conservative values creating experiences of rejection and conflict (Halkitis, Mattis, Sahadath, Massie, Ladyzhenskaya, Pitrelli, Bonacci & Cowie, 2009). Given the cultural importance of religion and family, this rejection could be particularly devastating. Thus, sexually marginalized individuals have been found to gravitate towards spirituality, focusing on their relationships with God, higher powers, self, others, sexual orientation integration and morality (Halkitis et al., 2009; Rodriguez & Ouellette, 2000). However, research on Latinx religiosity and sexual orientation rejection has focused on issues of gay men, *machismo* and masculinity rather than bisexual women.

Familism
Family or familism is a critical factor within Latinx culture. Familism, emphasizes loyalty, solidarity, interdependence and is core for Latinx communities (Acosta, 2010). These relationships are foundational to shaping intra and interpersonal characteristics of Latinx individuals (Sue & Sue, 2012). Creating consistent core values within self and role in the family. Further, Latinx families do not just include the nuclear family, but include extended family members as well. These members also play a significant role in raising children, providing resources, family finances and decision making (Cauce & Domenench-Rodriguez, 2002). Most importantly, families encompass a form of emotional and social support that buffers negative life circumstances such as substance abuse (Castro & Alarcon, 2002) and psychological distress (Stein, Gonzalez, Cuptio, Kiang & Supple, 2015). Disconnecting from this value could result in isolation and loss of crucial support systems.

Familism and Disclosure of Sexual Identity
For bisexual Latinx individuals, a common narrative in relation to familism is disclosure of sexual identity. Lesbian and bisexual Latinxs have

been found to disclose their identity to family, co-workers and communities than other ethnicities (Pastrana, 2015). Reasons involve having a strong sense of family support and major need, such as finances (Morris, Waldo, & Rothblum, 2001; Meyer, 2010). However, Acosta (2010), argues that if families are rejecting when a family member comes out, they are manipulative and controlling to protect traditional family values. Thus, concealment may be used to avoid facing fear of stigmatization, sexism and maintain family homeostasis (Hirai, Winkel, & Popen, 2014). For example, marginalized Latinx women engage in romantic relationships by pretending they are in relationships with men (Acosta, 2010).

This experience is reinforced to avoid being targeted as having no interest in childbearing because of their sexuality (Matthews & Selvidge, 2003) and avoid racism or sexism from family and communities (Balsam et al., 2011; Harper, Jernewall & Zea, 2004). Hence, is it worth coming out to their families or not? Unfortunately, this question and research has been absent without grouping bisexual Latinx women's experiences in with others, such as lesbian women. Thus, with limited and conflicting research findings, it would be beneficial to explore experiences of disclosure and family harmony.

Gender

Latinx women historically hold a subdued position within Latinx culture through labor, unequal earning, child bearing, earning potential and lack of economic independence (Acosta, 2010). This position may stem from culturally sanctioned gender roles, called *marianismo* for Latinx women (Miranda, Bilot, Peluso, Berman & Van Meek, 2006). Under *marianismo*, Latinx women are expected to raise and bear children, represent femininity, attend to primary needs of her husband, undermine her sexuality and reflect passivity (Low & Organista, 2000; Miranda et al., 2006). A potential source of gender norms revolves around continuation of family lineage (Ackerland & Chueng, 2000) and transitioning of gender roles as new generations come along (Blau, Kahn, Liu & Papps, 2013).

This treatment usually begins at a younger age and are held throughout a lifetime. Studies of Latinx culture and household norms, have found that boys and girls were treated differently, such as boys were granted more freedom, girls were encouraged to portray "feminine" behavior (i.e., cooking, feminine attire, politeness) and were kept under stricter parental regulation than their brothers (Céspedes, & Huey, 2008; Raffaelli & Ontai, 2004). As women get older and adhere to gender norms, the higher family cohesion, psychological well-being and less conflict they experience (Lorenzo-Blanco, Unger, Baezconde-Garbanati, Ritt-Olson & Soto, 2012). Women who have challenged gender norms have experienced resistance and unique intersecting struggles of ethnicity and gender (Cammarota, 2004; Sokoloff & Dupont, 2005). Leaving these women to potentially be targets of discrimination, oppression and victimization for deviation of the norm.

Gender and Bisexual Latinx Women

Gender factors in Latinx culture leave bisexual Latinx women at a disadvantage. Particularly, this community may experience microaggressions from Latinx culture and sexual marginalized communities (Balsam et al., 2011). Due to romantic engagement with both genders, bisexual women may be seen as a threat to feminism and resistance to oppressional systemic patriarchy, resulting in high tension with the bisexual community (McLean, 2008; Gehart, 2014). Bisexual Latinx women have further received intolerance and challenging from the lesbian community as bisexual women are viewed as "confused" or "greedy" (Nadal, Wong, Issa, Meterko, Leon & Wideman, 2011). Further, young men have also been found to prescribe bisexual Latinas as "highly sexual" or "slutty" (Chimiwelski, 2017). Lastly, bisexual women have been victims of over-eroticization due to heterosexual male attitudes of sexual fluidity (Worthen, 2013) and Latinx women have been perceived as sexually available to men and exotic (McCabe, 2009). Thus, multiple oppressed identities leave bisexual Latinx women in constant defense and exposure to discrimination in ethnic, sexually marginalized and dominant communities.

METHODS

This study utilized a qualitative approach to explore experiences of bisexual Latinx women and their relation to minority stress experiences according to Meyer's (2003) minority stress model. Specifically, the aim of this study was to highlight narratives focusing on Latinx cultural factors (religion, familism and gender). Research has begun to address the need to include ethnic, sexually marginalized individuals (Meyer, 2010). Yet, this action has lacked in minority stress research and research overall. This study used thematic analysis to examine themes regarding cultural factors and their relationship to the minority stress model for bisexual Latinx women. The following three research questions were addressed within a minority stress model construct:

Q1. What are the patterns that emerge regarding familism, religion and gender of bisexual Latinx women?

Q2. What stories and patterns emerge regarding navigations of identity?

Q3. What are the stories regarding ameliorative factors experienced of bisexual Latinx women?

Participants

Participants were 10 self-identified bisexual cis-gender women between the ages of 18 and 35 years old. All participants identified as Latinx, most identified as Mexican (n = 7), and others identified as Dominican (n = 1), Mexican/Dominican (n = 1) and Venezuelan (n = 1). All women had come out to at least one family member and identified as coming from a Catholic home but do not practice Catholicism to date. Eight women identified living in the Midwest, one was from Texas and another from New York. To protect confidentiality, participants are coded as "BL#" (See Table 1).

Table 1. Descriptive Demographics of Participant's Sample

Participant ID (age)	Ethnicity	Region	"Is your family religious?"
BL1 (21)	Mexican	West Coast	Disagree
BL2 (20)	Mexican	Midwest	Agree
BL3 (31)	Mexican	Southwest	Agree
BL4 (18)	Mexican	West Coast	Agree
BL5 (19)	Mexican	Midwest	Disagree
BL6 (24)	Dominican	Midwest	Agree
BL7 (29)	Mexican	Midwest	Agree
BL8 (30)	Venezuelan/Dominican	East Coast	Agree
BL9 (19)	Mexican	Midwest	Disagree
BL10 (22)	Mexican	Southwest	Agree

Inclusion criteria included being an age of 18 and older, identifying as Latinx, (Afro-Caribbean, Caribbean, Latina or Latino, which falls under Latinx terminology), bisexual and having disclosed their sexual orientation to at least one family member. This study involved identifying as bisexual to allow for experiences unique to this community. Thus, avoiding grouping sexually marginalized women such as women who have sex with women (WSW), queer or lesbian women who have different experiences (Martin & Pallotta-Chiarolli, 2009). Those who did not meet this criteria were excluded from this study.

Recruitment

Convenience and snowball sampling methods were used in qualitative participant recruitment. These methods allowed for easy accessibility and geographical proximity, especially for such an underrepresented population (Etikan, Musa & Alkassim, 2016). Convenience sampling, sampling that is available to the research by virtue of accessibility (Bryman, 2015), was optimal to utilize in this study. The researcher recruited participants through a variety of Latinx and lesbian, gay, bisexual, transgender and queer (LGBTQ) focused groups on social media (Facebook), and sent emails/flyers to Latinx and LGBTQ campus resource centers using the Centerlink community network (https://www.lgbtcenters.org/). Potential participants filled out a demographic screening questionnaire using Qualtrics and were contacted by the researcher, if eligible. To include snowball sampling methods, the researcher asked participants to forward information about the study to other potential or interested individuals. Snowball sampling is effective in qualitative recruitment as concerns of replication and generalization are less of a concern (Bryman, 2015).

Procedure

Once participants went to the online Qualtrics link, they were first informed of the purposes of the study with a consent page. Before answering demographic questions, participants acknowledged they fell within inclusion criteria (18 years old or older, identified as Latinx, bisexual, and disclosed sexual identity to at least one family member). Once they completed the demographic survey, including times and a phone number to call, the researcher contacted eligible participants via a telephone in a locked, secure office. Once contacted, the researcher discussed the consent form, research procedure, questions included in the interview and addressed any questions before the interview began. Participants were audio-recorded and interviews did not last longer than 45 minutes. The researcher thanked the participants and once again reiterated consent.

Interview

A semi-structured interview process with 11 open-ended questions was used for participants to provide detailed perspectives, adhere to their voices and not be influenced by leading questions. Specifically, these questions were formulated and communicated to avoid giving participants ques to expected answers (Merriam & Tisdell, 2016). Some questions within this interview included, "How would you describe religiosity in your family?

How would gender be described in your culture? How do you navigate your gender, sexual identity and ethnic identity?" Due to the sensitive nature of questions, including acceptance and identity navigation, the researcher included emergency hotline numbers in the consent form and repeated voluntary participation during the interview.

Demographic Questionnaire

A demographic questionnaire was used to gather information about participants' age, gender, ethnicity, native language, and religion.

Analytic Strategy

Data analysis was completed via thematic analysis of responses provided by bisexual Latinx women in this study. To ensure analytic thoroughness, the analytic process will be explicitly discussed and Braun and Clark's (2006) thematic analysis model was used. The process of analysis began by replaying audio interviews and transcribing them via transcription software onto a computer. For initial coding, the researcher read over the interviews for an open coding process. Through this process, the researcher kept an open mind and highlighted what stood out in relation to research questions. Initial codes were then generated from open codes. After clarification of initial codes, axial coding was conducted and inputted into a coding tree.

Coding trees are a significant piece to qualitative analysis, creating opportunity for an integration of structure and narrative to emerge (Merriam & Tisdell, 2016). Themes and subthemes were created from this tree using a minority stress construct. Themes were then defined as proximal stress: concealment among family, distal stress: gender discrimination and religiosity, and ameliorative factor: religious identity. Subthemes were defined as restricted expression, movement from family to friends, not enough, religious beliefs, invisibility, religious rejection, religious separation and self-discovery (See Table 2). The themes were then written and finalized by the researcher.

Trustworthiness

With qualitative data, how people interpret experiences, give meaning to their lives and construct their world is interpreted by the researcher (Merriam & Tisdell, 2016). Thus, it is important for readers to understand the researcher and her influence in this study. The researcher identifies as a Latinx lesbian cisgender woman and has extensive experience working with this community. She has interest in sexually marginalized Latinx research and has worked clinically with individuals, couples and families. The researcher also has an orientation toward social justice, cultural competency and advocacy research for underrepresented communities. Further, she has been on several qualitative research projects, both in research teams and being sole author.

Table 2. Thematic Themes of Bisexual Latinx Experiences and Minority Stress

Themes	Subthemes
Proximal Stress	Restricted Expression
	Movement from Family to Friends
	Noth Enough
Distral Stress	Religiosity
	Religious Beliefs
	Invisibility
	Religious Rejection
Ameliorative Factors	Religious Separation
	Self-Discovery

RESULTS

The results of this study portrays intersectionality and navigation for bisexual Latinx women in relation to the minority stress model. Four themes and eight subthemes emerged among the ten participants surrounding religiosity, familism and gender (See Table 2). These themes fell under specific minority stress concepts including proximal stress, distal stress and ameoraltive factors. First, women shared experiences of concealment of their sexual identity with their family but could express their sexuality with their friends. However, this navigation brought up feelings of inadequacy and loneliness. Second, women expressed experiences of discrimination due to their sexuality, gender and rejection from highly religious families. These experiences resulted in feelings of invisibility. Finally, religiosity also played a dual purpose of being an ameliorating factor in self-discovery. Participants reported moving away from religious practices and adapting their own spiritual identities as bisexual Latinx women.

Proximal Stress: Concealment among Family

Restricted Expression

A majority of participants (n = 9), shared that navigating and expressing their sexual and gender identity is a balancing act, a lot of which depends on their location and environment. Many shared commonalities of knowing how to act (i.e., not bring up their sexual orientation and feminine expression) around their families. Seven women expressed less freedom and comfort in expressing sexual orientation around their family than their friends. Expression including clothing, mannerisms, speaking of partners, activities and friends belonging to sexually marginalized communities. For example, Bisexual Latinx 4 shared, "I know for a fact that I can't bring up my girlfriend or that I am the vice-president to the LGBTQ club on campus to my parents. They would have a heart attack! So, I just pretend I haven't met anyone special and I don't speak of the club. Bisexual Latinx 2 expressed similar notions of restricted conversation, "I feel like in my family it's one of those things that has been very under like down low…we just don't talk about it and I don't bring it up."

Participants of the group gave unique reasons to conceal or restrict their sexual identity around their family. Some women spoke of making conscious choice of concealment at home rather than being authentically themselves to keep family stability. For example, Bisexual Latinx 8 shared, "I don't want to create fights or conflict when I go home, I barely go home anyway, so it is just better to keep my identity to myself." Bisexual Latinx 6 expressed that to her family is, "important to me, in Latino culture, especially Dominicans, we were raised that family is first. I can't break that bond no matter who I am attracted to." Bisexual Latinx 7 expresses that these beliefs and her family unit could be very abusive, and utilizes an ultimate form of concealment: disconnection.

> "The family culture is a lot of abuse, if you are not okay with that and you say something not typical, you are kind of rejected. It is the same if you are queer... they are so aggressive and will force you to be in a relationship with someone of the opposite sex...I am not in connections or communications with my family dealing with that."

Movement from Family to Friends

A quarter of women (n = 4) use concealment to prioritize significance of relationships and authenticity of their sexuality. For example, Bisexual Latinx 7 shared, "I mean, I know I am bisexual, my friends know I am bisexual, that is what matters. I let my parents keep trying to hook me up with *cabrones*, I know I'm not going on the dates so no harm done!" Bisexual Latinx 9 also shares friendships versus family authenticity, "Around my family at home, I usually never bring up anything about my sexual identity...around my friends and away from my family, I can just be me." These women also spoke of acceptance and openness with friendships. For example, Bisexual Latinx 1 expressed,

> "So, in regards to being with my family...yeah sexual identity, I don't really display much, we don't talk about it...it's just not focused on when I'm with my family. I don't really feel comfortable...then around friends...I can openly display all aspects of myself and that's when I feel I can be the most open and fully accepted so there's really no limitation as to what I can and can't express when I'm with them."

Not Enough

Three women described that concealing their identity and navigating their identities with their families, sexually marginalized communities and friendships, created feelings of inadequacy. Bisexual Latinx 10 shares her experience of loneliness that occurs from assumptions when not fitting in,

"It can be very lonely, trying to figure out how to act in front of my family, what not to say and what not. Then how to act in front of my [White] friends, I can't talk about my Latina problems. No one really understands." Bisexual Latinx 2 describes also describes her struggle with how she must portray a certain way.

> "I feel like some of the stress I have felt its been more about not being queer enough or Latino enough. It can be a real struggle you know...I have to portray a certain way of being Latina with my family and folks have thoughts on how queer folks should look like and I don't fit that."

Bisexual Latinx 9 expresses a similar struggle, "It's like the Selena movie, you have to be Mexican enough for the Mexicans, American enough for the Americans but with me you have to be gay enough for the gays, it is exhausting!"

Distral Stress: Gender Discrimination

Non-Existent Sexuality

A majority of participants, (n = 8) shared experiences of discrimination targeting their sexuality and gender. For example, Bisexual Latina 5 describes, "As a woman, I have faced harassment. But I think that is something that a lot of women face. But for me, I have had guys up to my face ask, "Which one do you prefer, you have to pick and not be greedy" and Bisexual Latinx 10 shares, "People never accept me doing it [dating women]...men have asked me to sleep with them, say they can keep me straight...its awful". Surprisingly, five women described experiences of discrimination from men, two of which were from the gay community. Bisexual Latinx 6 describes being taken advantage of because she was a woman, "I have gone to a gay bar and my breasts were groped by a gay man... So I view them [gay bars] in a different way" and bisexual Latinx 9 shares, "I even had a gay ex-friend grab me by my privates and tell me that if I was turned on by this, then I need a man not a woman".

Women described the basis of discrimination as "assumptions" and "phases", such as assuming *why* they identify as bisexual. Bisexual Latinx 3 shares, "People think I am doing it for attention…They just constantly say, "Oh you're just having fun, you're doing it for attention, you're exotic, you're Latina." Another women expressed this assumption in sharing, "We had Latino dances on campus, and we were all really aware if the girls were dancing together. So if we tried to dance together we were harassed for putting on a performance for them [men]."

Invisibility

Two women discussed the theme of sexual identity invisibility. Bisexual Latinx 2 expresses the invisibility of her sexuality, "My sister swears it's a phase and pretends it's not real," and bisexual Latinx 5 shares, "People try to erase my identity, they think I am a lesbian and I have to explain all the time that I am bi."

Distal Stress: Religiosity

Religious Beliefs

Overwhelmingly, all participants reported that their families were Catholic and held common religious practices while they were growing up in their home, even if their homes were not overwhelmingly religious. Bisexual Latinx 2 shared, "I was mainly Catholic and we would go to church a lot and every Sunday and for major holidays, we do a rosary…I didn't really grow up in a very religious home but there's always religion where having to go to church, being a good Catholic person." Bisexual Latinx 1 further describes religiosity in her family as, "Catholic and so obviously I would go to church every Sunday, we don't eat meat on certain days, my parents would say don't lose your virginity until you're married." Other practices expressed by bisexual Latinx 4 are being, "very involved in church, we went to the confirmation classes, we went to the masses, my parents were involved in the sermons and we were also in the choir." Other women noted what religion meant for their family. For example, bisexual Latinx 10 shared,

> "Religion for my family, as much as I don't agree with it now, was a way for us to be together and connect as a family," and bisexual Latinx 6 expressed, "Religion is just a Latino family thing...it's what you do."

Religious Rejection

Most bisexual Latinas noted consequences when custom religious practices were not followed, such as not identifying as heterosexual. Bisexual Latinx 7 shares, "When my mom found out, she bought these books about how if your child is not straight then it is a punishment for your sins. A whole series of books that have been translated from English to Spanish...she latched on to "Oh you're not straight so you must have demons or something." Another woman, bisexual Latinx 8, shared that "Coming out as bisexual, lesbian, gay or whatever, is a straight up sin. Probably forever unforgivable in the Latino culture." Five women discussed how religiosity impacted their family's acceptance of themselves and other family members. For example, bisexual Latinx 4 shares, "I haven't told them [parents] because from what happened with my sister. They reacted so negatively to her, it broke my heart and their only reason is because of their hard-core Catholicism...it has really been traumatizing," and bisexual Latinx 2 remarked, "My grandparents don't accept it, they're old and religious." Religious value goes so far as Bisexual Latinx 5 noted,

> "Because of religion and preserving marriage between a man and a woman is so sacred in my family, I have an uncle who pretends to be straight, is in a marriage with a woman and have children but they are in relationships with others of the same sex."

Ameliorative Factor: Religious Identity

Religious Separation and Self Discovery

A common theme from all participants was moving away from the traditional religion [Catholicism] and defining their own religious identity.

For five women, integrating their own beliefs with their authentic selves proved to be factors of self discovery. Bisexual Latinx 1 describes her experience as discovering her own spirituality after leaving home and her family for college, "I have to say I have my own spirituality so I don't really go to church every Sunday…in the mornings I do meditation and it's more goal focused.. just having my own personal connection with God." Another woman, bisexual Latinx 10, shares a similar experience finding other outlets for spiritual connections, "I have my own spiritual connection with our higher being I think. I don't practice anymore like my family does but that doesn't mean I don't have my faith." As some bisexual Latinxs described their own journeys of spirituality, others described reasons why they also have moved away from the religion their family practices [Catholicism] and differing from her family beliefs. For example, bisexual Latinx 4 remarked,

> "I do not really go to church anymore once we left home. The rules are so strict, the woman and man have to be together is all they say…So now I feel that we are different from our family because we do not identify as hard core Catholic anymore but that is fine, there are different ways of practicing it."

Bisexual Latinx 7 described her faith versus her mother's, "Religion always seemed very foreign to me. My mother's faith always seems like my mother's faith not mine. To her it justified her own behavior but to me, it didn't make sense to how they reacted or conventional." Similarly, bisexual Latinx 3 expressed understanding is essential to separate sexuality and religion, "I'm not very religious so I don't think it really effects me. But I respect everyone's own opinions and beliefs…You have to understand that everyone had differing views on religion and sexuality."

CONCLUSION

The findings of this study highlight unique intersecting narratives of bisexual Latinx women and how they fit into the minority stress model. Prior to this study, studies of bisexual women have proven to be scarce, bisexual

Latinx women were largely missing from empirical literature and experiences of these women in the minority stress model is absent (Meyer, 2010). Thus, utilizing a minority stress concept and an intersectional lens to understand their experiences, is important to fill gaps in literature and for other reasons. First, navigating multiple marginalized identities of bisexual Latinas constitutes a balancing act around their families. Familism is a core value within Latinx culture (Acosta, 2010), and ways of maintaining family harmony creates a backstory to how significant family is. This fact is notable in participants descriptions of concealment through lack of intimate discussions of their sexuality to avoid conflict and emphasize family bond in Latinx culture. This supports literature describing how concealment is used to maintain family homeostasis, avoid stigmatization and can be adapted into the minority stress model (Hiraiet al., 2014; Meyer, 2003).

In relation to the minority stress model, participants discussed concealing and open expression to their friendships. They are unable to express authentically to their families; thus their friendships take priority. Thus, moving away from traditionally relying on emotional and social support on family members, and relying on their friendships (Miranda, Bilot, Berman & Van Meek, 2006). From identity navigation, family and friendships, and concealment, participants discussed feelings of loneliness and inadequacy. Particularly, not being enough for each community (Latinx and sexually marginalized). Furthering supporting research of psychological distress from identity navigation and internal conflicts (Bowleg, Huang, Brooks, Black & Burkholder, 2003).

Second, discrimination was reported in multiple faucets involving gender, sexuality and religion. A majority of participants described experiences of discrimination from men, gay and straight, demeaning their sexuality as non-existent. These experiences fall under distal stressors within the minority stress model and relate to, unfortunately, common experiences of bisexual women (Balsam & Szymanski, 2005; Bostwick et al., 2010). Further, these results suggest experiences of invisibility these women also experience, as literature has also found (Barker & Langdridge, 2008) Yet, unique to these women, are their narratives of ethnic experiences intersecting with discrimination such as being stereotyped as "exotic" and sexualized for male pleasure (Lopez, 2013).

Third, religiosity was reported to be a core Latinx cultural factor for each participant describing practices involving church, holiday, rosaries, choir, attending masses and marriage principles. These practices are described as not just acts but a component of connection and an understood expectation for Latinx families. Supporting continued beliefs, foundations of Latinx culture and adherence to tradition significance (García et al., 2008). Surprisingly, most participants discussed the consequences of identifying as bisexual with religious families and the impact it has on family acceptance of their sexual identities; relating to distal stress. Unique to these participants, are the narratives of how religiosity has traumatized experiences before coming out, coming out the coming out of their family members. Yet, despite the stress religiosity enacts for these women, they shared experiences of moving away from traditional religiosity and creating their own religious identity. Thus, creating a unique journey of self-discovery, empowerment and an ameliorative factor to coping with minority stressors (Meyer, 2015). Which supports research portraying a movement away from conservative, traditional religious value and adherence to liberal religious value instead (Diaz-Stevens, 2018).

Overall through narratives, these results suggest imperative Latinx cultural factors that should be considered within the minority stress model. Without the voices of bisexual Latinx women, multicultural research will continue to stay stagnant. This study brings to the light bisexual Latinx experiences of cultural and identity navigation that steers their daily lives. Participants in this study reflected depth and complexity of their experiences. Importantly, these experiences were able to be translated into the minority stress model to aid inclusivity and expand understanding of this community. Through ethnic, sexual and gender oppression --- inflicted by a predominantly patriarchal White society, a traditional Latinx society, and a static sexually marginalized community, --- these women still thrive and navigate their identities.

The results and implications of this study are cautioned by selection bias. Bisexual Latinx participants were recruited from across the country through

Facebook ads, emails or flyers directed towards the LGBTQ Latinx community. Both convenience and snowball sampling methods have limitations in bias of participants, possibility of outliers and unpredictability of samples (Etikan et al., 2016). Further, almost all of the women were in liberal college environments and to ensure confidentiality, self reported identities were not verified. This study also recognizes a majority of participants are of Mexican decent and may have different experiences than other Latinx communities. Thus, grouping and overrepresentation is reflected here (Gehart, 2014). Finally, the researcher conducted sole qualitative analysis, incorporating possible researcher bias without other perspectives to discuss results with. For future directions, it would be beneficial to obtain a variety of participants from different avenues of life to fully grasp experiences of bisexual Latinxs as a whole. Also, this study takes accounts from these women of their families. It would increase in depth exploration to include family perspectives in understanding family systems.

Bisexual Latinx women have learned to create and integrate multiple marginalized identities from constant fluxing environments; at times facing loss of self, society and their families during the process. Their enduring narratives are especially instructive to expand intersectionality and minority stress theory. Also, the complexity of navigating and dynamically shifting identities should not be taken for granted. It is imperative to comprehend the dominant narratives that must be hidden at times, depending on their environments. Understanding power constructs in a White, heterosexist society would be useful in considering how safe these environments are for identity navigation. Bisexual Latinx women are going against the grain as Latinx women are historically based off submissive, *marinismo* traditions (Acosta, 2010). The need to empower these women is essential, as they face multiple oppressive environments. Finally, literature thoroughly discusses mental health outcomes of sexually marginalized communities (Meyer, 2003), yet, understanding lacks on mental health outcomes for bisexual Latinx women. This study provides a piece of that context and the emotions that fill experiences of these women. Based on these experiences, invisibility, loneliness and inadequacy are constant mental health issues that needs to be grasped by society to benefit this marginalized community. Bisexual Latinx 5 captures this need best,

> "Rather than just having a genuine interest in who the person is or just focusing on their gender. I just want someone to appreciate me and love me for the way I am."

REFERENCES

Acosta, K. (2010). "How could you do this to me?": How lesbian, bisexual, and queer Latinas negotiate sexual identity with their families. *Black Women, Gender & Families, 4*(I). Retrieved from https://muse.jhu.edu/article/380612.

Adames, H. Y., Chavez-Dueñas, N. Y., Sharma, S., & La Roche, M. J. (2018). Intersectionality in psychotherapy: The experiences of an Afro Latinx queer immigrant. *Psychotherapy, 55*(II): 73-79.

Akerlund, M., & Cheung, M. (2000). Teaching beyond the deficit model: Gay and lesbian issues among African Americans, Latinos, and Asian Americans. *Journal of Social Work Education, 36*(II): 279-292.

Arana, M. (2001). The elusive Hispanic/Latino identity. *Nieman Reports, 55*(II), 8-9.

Balsam, K. F., & Szymanski, D. M. (2005). Relationship quality and domestic violence in women's same-sex relationships: the role of minority stress. *Psychology of Women Quarterly, 29*(III): 258-269.

Balsam, K. F., Molina, Y., Beadnell, B., Simoni, J., & Walters, K. (2011). Measuring multiple minority stress: The LGBT people of color microaggressions scale. *Cultural Diversity and Ethnic Minority Psychology, 17*(II): 163-174.

Barker, M., & Langdridge, D. (2008). Bisexuality: Working with a silenced sexuality. *Feminism & Psychology, 18*(III):389-394.

Barker, M., Yockney, J., Richards, C., Jones, R., Bowes-Catton, H., & Plowman, T. (2012). Guidelines for researching and writing about bisexuality. *Journal of Bisexuality, 12*(III): 376-392.

Blau, F. D., Kahn, L. M., Liu, A. Y. H., & Papps, K. L. (2013). The transmission of women's fertility, human capital, and work orientation acrossimmigrant generations. *Journal of Population Economics, 26*(II): 405-435.

Bostwick, W. B., Boyd, C. J., Hughes, T. L., & McCabe, S. E. (2010). Sexual orientation and the prevalence of mood and anxiety disorders in the United States. *American Journal of Public Health, 100* (I): 468–475.

Bowleg, L., Huang, J., Brooks, K., Black, A., & Burkholder, G. (2003). Triple jeopardy and beyond: Multiple minority stress and resilience among Black lesbians. *Journal of Lesbian Studies, 7*(IV): 87-108.

Braun, V., & Clarke, V. (2006). Using thematic analysis in psychology. *Qualitative Research in Psychology, 3*(II): 77-101.

Bryman, A. (2015). *Social Research Methods (4th ed.)*. London, UK: Oxford University Press.

Cammarota, J. (2004). The gendered and racialized pathways of Latina and Latino youth: Different struggles, different resistances in the urban context. *Anthropology & Education Quarterly, 35*(I): 53-74.

Castro, F. G., & Alarcon, E. H. (2002). Integrating cultural variables into drug abuse prevention and treatment with racial/ethnic minorities. *Journal of Drug Issues, 32*(III): 783-810.

Cauce, A. M., & Domenech-Rodriguez, M. (2002). Latino families: Myths and realities. *Latino Children and Families in the United States: Current Research and Future Directions*, (I): 3-25.

Céspedes, Y. M., & Huey Jr, S. J. (2008). Depression in Latino adolescents: a cultural discrepancy perspective. *Cultural Diversity and Ethnic Minority Psychology, 14*(II): 168-172.

Chmielewski, J. F. (2017). A listening guide analysis of lesbian and bisexual young Women of Color's experiences of sexual objectification. *Sex Roles, 77*(VII-VIII): 533-549.

Cho, S., Crenshaw, K. W., & McCall, L. (2013). Toward a field of intersectionality studies: Theory, applications, and praxis. *Signs: Journal of Women in Culture and Society, 38*(IV): 785-810.

Cochran, S. D., Mays, V. M., Alegria, M., Ortega, A. N., & Takeuchi, D. (2007). Mental health and substance use disorders among Latino and

Asian American lesbian, gay, and bisexual adults. *Journal of Consulting and Clinical Psychology, 75*(V): 785–794.

Crenshaw, K. (1991). Mapping the margins: Intersectionality, identity politics, and violence against women of color. *Stanford Law Review*, (I): 1241-1299.

Davis, K. (2008). Intersectionality as buzzword: A sociology of science perspective on what makes a feminist theory successful. *Feminist theory, 9*(I): 67-85.

Diaz-Stevens, A. M. (2018). *Recognizing the Latino resurgence in US religion: The Emmaus paradigm.* New York, NY: Routledge.

Dutwin, D. (2012). LGBT acceptance and support: The Hispanic perspective. *Social Science Research Solutions*. Retrieved from www.ncir.org/images/uploads/publicagions/LGBTAS_HispanicPerspective.pdf.

García, D. I., Gray-Stanley, J., & Ramirez-Valles, J. (2008). "The priest obviously doesn't know that I'm gay": The religious and spiritual journeys of Latino gay men. *Journal of Homosexuality, 55*(III): 411-436.

Gehart, D. R. (2014). *Theory and Treatment Planning in Family Therapy: A Competency-based Approach.* San Francisco, CA: Cengage Learning.

Espinosa, G. (2008). The influence of religion on Latino education, marriage, and social views in the United States. *Marriage & Family Review, 43*(III-IV): 205-225.

Etikan, I., Musa, S. A., & Alkassim, R. S. (2016). Comparison of convenience sampling and purposive sampling. *American Journal of Theoretical and Applied Statistics, 5*(I): 1-4.

Frost, D. M., & Meyer, I. H. (2009). Internalized homophobia and relationship quality among lesbians, gay men, and bisexuals. *Journal of Counseling Psychology, 56*(I): 97-109.

Halkitis, P. N., Mattis, J. S., Sahadath, J. K., Massie, D., Ladyzhenskaya, L., Pitrelli, K., Bonacci & Cowie, S. A. E. (2009). The meanings and manifestations of religion and spirituality among lesbian, gay, bisexual, and transgender adults. *Journal of Adult Development, 16*(IV): 250-262.

Hamilton, C. J., & Mahalik, J. R. (2009). Minority stress, masculinity, and social norms predicting gay men's health risk behaviors. *Journal of Counseling Psychology, 56*(I): 132-141.

Harper, G. W., Jernewall, N., & Zea, M. C. (2004). Giving voice to emerging science and theory for lesbian, gay, and bisexual people of color. *Cultural Diversity and Ethnic Minority Psychology, 10*(III):187-199.

Hatzenbuehler, M. L., Nolen-Hoeksema, S., & Erickson, S. J. (2008). Minority stress predictors of HIV risk behavior, substance use, and depressive symptoms: results from a prospective study of bereaved gay men. *Health Psychology, 27*(IV): 455-462.

Hendricks, M. L., & Testa, R. J. (2012). A conceptual framework for clinical work with transgender and gender nonconforming clients: An adaptation of the Minority Stress Model. *Professional Psychology: Research and Practice, 43*(V): 460-467.

Herek, G. M., & Gonzalez-Rivera, M. (2006). Attitudes toward homosexuality among US residents of Mexican descent. *Journal of Sex Research, 43*(II): 122-135.

Hirai, M., Winkel, M. H., & Popan, J. R. (2014). The role of machismo in prejudice toward lesbians and gay men: Personality traits as moderators. *Personality and Individual Differences, 70*(I): 105-110.

Lehavot, K., & Simoni, J. M. (2011). The impact of minority stress on mental health and substance use among sexual minority women. *Journal of Consulting and Clinical Psychology, 79*(II): 159-170.

Logie, C. H., Newman, P. A., Chakrapani, V., & Shunmugam, M. (2012). Adapting the minority stress model: associations between gender non-conformity stigma, HIV-related stigma and depression among men who have sex with men in South India. *Social Science & Medicine, 74*(VIII): 1261-1268.

Lopez, J. P. (2013). Speaking with them or speaking for them: A conversation about the effect of stereotypes in the Latina/Hispanic women's experiences in the United States. *New Horizons in Adult Education and Human Resource Development, 25*(II): 99-106.

Lorenzo-Blanco, E. I., Unger, J. B., Baezconde-Garbanati, L., Ritt-Olson, A., & Soto, D. (2012). Acculturation, enculturation, and symptoms of depression in Hispanic youth: The roles of gender, Hispanic cultural values, and family functioning. *Journal of Youth and Adolescence, 41*(X):1350-1365.

Low, G., & Organista, K. C. (2000). Latinas and sexual assault: Towards culturally sensitive assessment and intervention. *Journal of Multicultural Social Work, 8*(I-II): 131-157.

Martin, E., & Pallotta-Chiarolli, M. (2009). 'Exclusion by inclusion': bisexual young people, of marginalisation and mental health in relation to substance abuse. In A. Taket, B. Crisp, A. Nevill, G. Lamaro, M. Graham, S. Barter-Godfrey (Eds,), *Theorising social exclusion*, (pp. 143-153). New York, NY: Routledge.

Merriam, S. B., & Tisdell, E. J. (2016). *Qualitative Research: A Guide to Design and Implementation.* San Francisco, CA: John Wiley & Sons, Inc.

Meyer, I. H. (2003). Prejudice, social stress, and mental health in lesbian, gay, and bisexual populations: conceptual issues and research evidence. *Psychological bulletin, 129*(V): 674-697.

Meyer, I. H. (2010). Identity, stress, and resilience in lesbians, gay men, and bisexuals of color. *The Counseling Psychologist, 38*(III): 442-454.

Meyer, I. H. (2015). Resilience in the study of minority stress and health of sexual and gender minorities. *Psychology of Sexual Orientation and Gender Diversity, 2*(III): 209-213.

McCabe, J. (2009). Racial and gender microaggressions on a predominantly-White campus: Experiences of Black, Latina/o and White undergraduates. *Race, Gender & Class*, (I): 133-151.

McCabe, S. E., Bostwick, W. B., Hughes, T. L., West, B. T., & Boyd, C. J. (2010). The relationship between discrimination and substance use disorders among lesbian, gay, and bisexual adults in the United States. *American Journal of Public Health, 100*(X): 1946-1952.

McLean, K. (2008). Inside, outside, nowhere: Bisexual men and women in the gay and lesbian community. *Journal of Bisexuality, 8*(I-II: 63-80.

Miranda, A. O., Bilot, J. M., Peluso, P. R., Berman, K., & Van Meek, L. G. (2006). Latino families: The relevance of the connection among acculturation, family dynamics, and health for family counseling research and practice. *The Family Journal, 14*(III): 268-273.

Morris, J. F., Waldo, C. R., & Rothblum, E. D. (2001). A model of predictors and outcomes of outness among lesbian and bisexual women. *American Journal of Orthopsychiatry, 71*(I): 61-71.

Nadal, K. L., Wong, Y., Issa, M. A., Meterko, V., Leon, J., & Wideman, M. (2011). Sexual orientation microaggressions: Processes and coping mechanisms for lesbian, gay, and bisexual individuals. *Journal of LGBT Issues in Counseling, 5*(I):21-46.

Pastrana, A. J. (2015). Being out to others: The relative importance of family support, identity and religion for LGBT Latina/os. *Latino Studies, 13*(I): 88-112.

Rodriguez, E. M., & Ouellette, S. C. (2000). Gay and lesbian Christians: Homosexual and religious identity integration in the members and participants of a gay-positive church. *Journal for the Scientific Study of Religion, 39*(III): 333-347.

Raffaelli, M., & Ontai, L. L. (2004). Gender socialization in Latino/a families: Results from two retrospective studies. *Sex Roles, 50*(V-VI): 287-299.

Ryan, C., Huebner, D., Diaz, R. M., & Sanchez, J. (2009). Family rejection as a predictor of negative health outcomes in White and Latino lesbian, gay and bisexual young adults. *Pediatrics, 123*(I): 346–352.

Ryan, C., Russell, S. T., Huebner, D., Diaz, R., & Sanchez, J. (2010). Family acceptance in adolescence and the health of LGBT young adults. *Journal of Child and Adolescent Psychiatric Nursing, 23*(IV): 205-213.

Skinner, D. G., Correa, V., Skinner, M., & Bailey Jr, D. B. (2001). Role of religion in the lives of Latino families of young children with developmental delays. *American Journal on Mental Retardation, 106*(IV): 297-313.

Sokoloff, N. J., & Dupont, I. (2005). Domestic violence at the intersections of race, class, and gender: Challenges and contributions to understanding violence against marginalized women in diverse communities. *Violence Against Women, 11*(I): 38-64.

Stein, G. L., Gonzalez, L. M., Cupito, A. M., Kiang, L., & Supple, A. J. (2015). The protective of familism in the lives of Latino adolescents. *Journal of Family Issues, 36*(X), 1255-1273.

Sue, D. W., & Sue, D. (2012). *Counseling the Culturally Diverse: Theory and Practice (7th ed.)*. Hoboken, NJ: John Wiley & Sons.

Worthen, M. G. (2013). An argument for separate analyses of attitudes toward lesbian, gay, bisexual men, bisexual women, MtF and FtM transgender individuals. *Sex Roles, 68*(VI-VII): 703-723.

In: Intersectionality
Editor: Thomas Moeller

ISBN: 978-1-53617-110-5
© 2020 Nova Science Publishers, Inc.

Chapter 3

ADDING INTERACTIONS IN ORDER TO MODEL INTERSECTIONALITY: AN EMPIRICAL STUDY ON SELF-PERCEIVED HEALTH STATUS IN ARGENTINA

Matías S. Ballesteros[*], *PhD and Mercedes Krause, PhD*
IIGG-UBA/CONICET & IIGG-UBA, Buenos Aires, Argentina

ABSTRACT

In recent decades, intersectionality has been at the center of both feminist debates and the theory of gender. In the United States, Canada and Europe, it has achieved a hegemonic status, strengthened by its multiple possible applications, precisely because it does not meet the necessary requirements to become a theory or conception with defined contours.

Intersectionality was mainly incorporated in qualitative studies, favoring methodologies that were deemed to be best suited to address the complexity which lies within (e.g., ethnography, deconstruction, genealogy, ethnomethodology and case studies). In the field of population health research in particular, new approaches to model intersectionality in quantitative studies are still emerging. One way of making progress in multivariate analysis has been to calculate logistic regressions models

---
[*] Corresponding author's E-mail: matiballesteros@yahoo.com.ar.

separately for men and for women. Other authors work with additive models from multiple linear regressions, where different "levels of intersectionality" are included in different steps of the regression. Another possible approach, when applying multiplicative models, is the inclusion of interaction terms in conventional regression models.

This chapter aims at contributing to these theoretical-methodological discussions about intersectionality throughout an empirical analysis of health inequalities in Argentina. More specifically, we use one of the many multiplicative statistical models to analyze the self-perceived health status of the population aged 18 and older, living in urban areas of Argentina. We address the effect of different sociodemographic and geographical variables on self-perceived health status, and then we add interactions within the regression: between gender and educational level, between gender and the income quintile and between gender and the age group. We work with the data of the National Survey of Risk Factors (ENFR for Encuesta Nacional de Factores de Riesgo in Spanish, 2013), provided jointly by the National Institute of Statistics and Censuses (INDEC) and the National Ministry of Health in Argentina (MSAL). This survey was carried out based on a probabilistic design (by conglomerates and stratified), throughout four stages (department, area, housing and household member). The final database is made up of 32,365 cases nationwide.

INTRODUCTION

In recent decades, intersectionality has been at the center of both feminist debates and the theory of gender. It has been remarked as the "most important theoretical contribution", in conjunction with related fields, that women's studies have accomplished so far (McCall 2005, 1771). In the United States, Canada and Europe, it has achieved a hegemonic status and it continues to gain popularity in Latin America. Ten years ago, Davis (2008) announced that intersectionality had become a spectacular phenomenon, whose success was strengthened due to its multiple possible applications, ambiguities and incompleteness. The new "buzzword" appealed not only to generalists –thanks to easy-to-remember clichés such as "asking the other question"[1]- but also to specialists interested in an old existing problem

---

[1] "Asking the other question" is the method proposed by Matsuda (1991, 1189, cited in Davis 2008, 70) to understand the interconnection between different forms of social subordination: "When I see something that looks racist, I ask, 'Where is the patriarchy in this?' When I see

within the feminist studies: grasping the complexities and differences between women (Davis 2008). It was precisely because intersectionality does not meet the necessary requirements to become a theory or conception with defined contours, that feminists of different organizations, disciplines, theoretical perspectives and political positions seemed to agree upon that it was just what they were looking for (Davis 2008, 68).

A decade later, the discussion about when, where and how to apply intersectional analysis has not been left behind. Its ambiguity as well as its open character are still productive and stimulating new ways of doing empirical analysis. For a while, intersectionality was mainly incorporated in qualitative studies, favoring methodologies that were deemed to be best suited to address the complexity which lies within (e.g., ethnography, deconstruction, genealogy, ethnomethodology and case studies). It has even been argued that the core of intersectionality –constituted by the interdependence, multidimensionality and mutually constitutive relationships that exist between inequality axes- is inherently opposed to most quantitative approaches (Bowleg 2008, 317)[2]. Other authors reckon the need for both new methodological strategies, as well as for quantitative empirical research to be up to date, in comparison with qualitative theoretical and empirical advances (McCall 2005, Bowleg 2012, Richman and Zucker 2019, among others).

Currently, there are emerging new statistical models -some very complex ones- so as to study intersectionality. However, the question of how intersectional analysis should be done is still a matter of widespread interest and debate. Consensus on the best ways to conduct quantitative intersectional research remains limited (Richman and Zucker 2019, 3). The interested parties in doing so "often have to self-teach and learn through trial and error" (Bowleg 2008, 313).

This chapter aims at contributing to these theoretical-methodological discussions about intersectionality throughout an empirical analysis of

---

something that looks sexist, I ask, 'Where is the heterosexism in this?' When I see something that looks homophobic, I ask, 'Where are the class interests in this?'".

[2] According to Else-Quest and Hyde (2016a, 160), this supposed incompatibility between intersectionality and quantitative methodology is based on necessarily associating quantitative research with positivist epistemology, which is incorrect.

health inequalities in Argentina. More specifically, our objective is to analyze the self-perceived health status using a multiplicative statistical model. It should be noted we understand that the possibility of doing intersectional analysis is equally related to both the theoretical interpretation of the data as well as to the implemented statistical techniques. Therefore, we first delineate what we would understand as an intersectional analysis (and what we would not). Secondly, we present the data of the third National Survey of Risk Factors and our methodological decisions. Thirdly, we address the effect of different sociodemographic and geographical variables on self-perceived health status, and then we add interactions within the regression: between gender and educational level, between gender and the income quintile and between gender and the age group. Finally, we discuss the results and conclude with an evaluation of its originality.

WHAT IS (AND WHAT IS NOT) AN INTERSECTIONAL ANALYSIS?

Intersectionality's ambiguity and open nature may stimulate researcher's creativity and initiative, but it also entails the danger of believing that "anything goes" (Warner 2016, 345). That is why, our next step is to review some forms of empirical analysis that we do not consider intersectional, so as to clear up the basic principles that any intersectional analysis should fulfill.

Much progress has been made in the fields of public health or population health studies when analyzing the social inequalities in health. However, many of these advances examine each axis of inequality as a distinct and independent dimension: e.g., inequalities in health by race or ethnicity, inequalities in health by gender, and inequalities in health by social class without taking into account a possible entanglement between them (Veenstra 2011, 1). This type of analysis is not intersectional because it fails to accomplish intersectionality's most elementary and theoretical principle, which is the notion that social categories (for example, race, social class, gender and sexuality) are multiple, interdependent and mutually constitutive (Bowleg 2012, 1268).

If we take a step further, we find numerous studies carried out from the perspective of the social determinants of health, which have even performed an analysis of statistical interactions among social categories within their regression models. However, these studies do not explicitly apply the theories of intersectionality when theoretically interpreting the results (Veenstra 2011, 3). Following Bowleg (2012, 1267), it is not a semantic issue but a theoretical and political one, given that a second basic principle of intersectional analysis seeks to make explicit that the intersections of multiple social identities at the microsocial level reflect both multiple and intertwined systems of inequality at the macro structural level. Intersectionality theorizes how the different relations of power and oppression make up a system of social stratification as a whole (Marecek 2016, 177). As a critical theory, it invites us to get rid of the idea of a neutral and apolitical science, and instead, to use analysis for the empowerment of oppressed groups and individuals in order to eradicate social inequities (Else-Quest and Hyde 2016a, 2016b, 158, Warner et al. 2016, 173, Richman and Zucker 2019, 8). Therefore, Richman and Zucker (2019, 1) warn us: when using the tools of statistical analysis, it is important not to lose sight of the origins and the historical foundations of intersectionality, which made up their inherent transforming spirit. From an intersectional standpoint, the results of the analysis should be interpreted within a social, historical and structural inequality context (Else-Quest 2016a, 164).

Far from complying with these principles, many studies of the social determinants of health, do not name intersectionality as a phenomenon of interest, and, more importantly, they do not refer to the relations of power and oppression that underlie the interaction between variables. They rely, instead, that variables such as race, gender, sexual orientation, social class and disability are explanatory constructions within themselves (Bowleg 2008, 322).

In short, we agree with Else-Quest and Hyde (2016a) on the point that intersectionality is more than just a statistical model. Characterizing the demographic differences or comparing the different social groups is not enough to achieve an intersectional analysis; rather, it is the analysis and interpretation of results within both, a socio-historical context and an inequality structure, that might best define intersectional research (Bowleg 2008, 323). Thus, it would be a mistake to think that the lack of statistically significant interactions invalidates or refutes the idea that different identities and social positions intersect themselves, or are coproduced and experienced simultaneously (Evans 2019, 26). In this sense, it is worth remembering that intersectionality should be considered as an analytical framework rather than a theory to be tested or rejected in the positivist sense (Else-Quest and Hyde 2016a, 159). For example, Aguilar et al. (2016, 145) aims to analyze the effect of the intersection between class and gender on the quality of employment in Chile. They postulate as their own hypothesis, that the condition of being a woman could act as an "amplifying mechanism" of class differences in the objective and subjective indexes of employment quality. Based on logistic regressions for men and for women separately, they reject the hypothesis and therefore conclude the following:

> "The foregoing does not mean that gender is not a mechanism of fundamental importance in understanding how inequality in the labour market is generated or functions (…) Overall, these results suggest that both class and gender play a central role in the perpetuation of inequalities in the Chilean labour market. They also indicate that, in some cases, gender is a fundamental consideration in understanding how class-based inequalities operate or, in this specific case, how social class influences subjective aspects of job quality, such as the perception of control over work processes" (Aguilar et al. 2016, 149).

Finally, it has been argued that describing "multiple main effects" is a valid strategy of intersectional analysis. Else-Quest and Hyde (2016b, 329) expose the following example:

> "Continuing with the example from Method 3.A with stratified random sampling that produces a 2 (Gender) x 3 (Race) quasi-experimental design with roughly equal numbers of participants in each cell or group, suppose the outcome variable is self-esteem; the analysis would examine main effects of both gender and race. From an intersectionality framework, those statistical results would be interpreted as indicating that both race and gender are linked to self-esteem".

The inclusion of this strategy as valid intersectional approach is certainly controversial. We agree with Bowleg and Bauer (2016, 339) that this type of analysis studies the effects of gender and race on self-esteem as mutually exclusive, without addressing the intersection between gender and race and, therefore, represents exactly what has been criticized as an additive approach towards social inequalities.

Now, what models of analysis can serve to account these intersectionality theories? Without intending to be exhaustive, here are some of the most implemented models. A first and simple variant in which one can work with simple statistical techniques such as bivariate tables, consists of constructing categories that represent intersections (for example, working class black man, middle class white woman) and see what effects they have on the dependent variable (Bauer and Scheim 2019, 238). Now moving to multivariate analyzes, one way of making progress has been to calculate logistic regressions models separately for men and for women. This is how authors from the European social epidemiology address the subject (Rohlfs et al. 2000, Artazcoz et al. 2001, Borrell and Artazcoz 2008, García Calvente et al. 2010), which has been replicated in Argentina by Krause and Ballesteros (2018). Other authors work with additive models from multiple linear regressions, where different "levels of intersectionality" are included in different steps of the regression (Seng et al. 2012). Another possible approach is the inclusion of interaction terms in conventional regression models (Veenstra 2011, Ballesteros 2018) and multilevel models (Evans, 2019).

METHODOLOGY

This chapter is based on the quantitative analysis of secondary data. The implemented statistical source is the third National Survey of Risk Factors (ENFR for Encuesta Nacional de Factores de Riesgo in Spanish) conducted during 2013 by the National Institute of Statistics and Censuses (INDEC) and the National Ministry of Health in Argentina (MSAL). It was carried out based on a multistage probabilistic design (by conglomerates and stratified), throughout four stages (department, area, housing and household member) and it allows to perform estimation for population living in urban areas of Argentina with 5000 inhabitants and more. The final database is made up of 32,365 cases nationwide.

In order to analyze existing inequalities in health, we examine the indicator of self-perceived health status. The variable is divided in five categories: excellent, very good, good, fair and poor. We dichotomized the variable grouping excellent and very good health statuses, and good, fair and poor health statuses. Several epidemiological studies have shown that the reported self-perception of health status can serve as a good predictor of population's health status, its morbidity, its disability and its mortality. Self-perceived health status is generally used as a proxy for objective and subjective health status in local and international studies (Ocampo 2010). We begin by performing a bivariate analysis between this dependent variable and the household income quintile per consumer unit, as well as the educational level, the gender, the age group and the region of residence[3]. Then we incorporate all the previous variables in a binary logistic regression. From the logistic regression, we can find out the effect of an independent variable on the dependent one, once the rest of the independent variables are controlled. For example, it can unveil us the net effect of gender on the odds of having a positive self-perceived health status, once a set of other variables have been controlled (such as age, household income, educational level and region of residence). However, it fails to show whether, for example, gender differences remain constant among people belonging to households of diverse incomes, educational levels or age groups. In order to test this hypothesis of intersectionality between variables, we incorporate into the regressions, the following interactions between gender and educational level, between gender and income quintile and between gender and age group. We do not include any variable on race or ethnicity, just because neither the ENFR 2013, nor the great majority of the surveys conducted in

---

[3] The household income per consumer unit arises from the division between the total household income (numerator) and the square root of the number of household members (denominator). Unlike the per capita income of the household where the simple sum of the members of the household is located in the denominator, this indicator takes into account that "economies of scale derived from family life" share resources (MSAL, 2015: 58).

Argentina, actually inquire about this issue. It should be noted that the interaction between gender and race or ethnicity, is one of the most applied in intersectional analysis (Evans 2019, 15).

We emphasize that social inequalities in the self-perception of health status have been analyzed through different models in Argentina. The majority of these studies could be framed within the additive models towards social inequalities, and they explore the effect that different independent variables have on the self-perception of health status. Some use bivariate and trivariate tables (MSAL 2006, 2011, 2015, Adaszko 2011, Observatorio de la Deuda Social Argentina 2015, Rodríguez Espínola and Filgueira 2018). Others use binary logistic regressions (Jorrat et al. 2008, MSAL 2012, Ballesteros 2014, Sarti and Rodríguez Espinosa 2018) and multilevel regressions (Alazraqui et al. 2009). Fewer studies have incorporated models of multiplicative analysis, appointing gender as the central variable. These are based on trivariate tables in which gender is considered a control variable (López et al. 2005) as well as on differential logistic regressions for men and for women (Krause and Ballesteros 2018). Thus, applying our model of analysis to the case of Argentina is truly groundbreaking, given that none of these antecedents incorporates interactions within regressions.

RESULTS

In Table 1 we present the bivariate relationship between self-perceived health status and a set of independent variables. Table 1 evidences that the highest percentages of the population with excellent or very good self-perceived health status are among those who have completed higher education (52.6%), among members of households in the 5th. income quintile (48.6%), among people who reside in Buenos Aires City (46.1%), among men (38.5%) and among those who belong to the youngest age group (53.1%). On the contrary, the level of excellent or very good self-perceived health status is low among households in the 1st. quintile of income (27.3%), among the population that completed less than elementary school (16.7%), among women (33.6%) and among people aged 65 and older (16.6%). By regions, residents of the Northeast (28.7%), of Buenos Aires suburban area (30.0%) and of the Northwest (31.5%) have lower levels of self-perceived health status than residents of other regions. In other words, excellent or very good self-perceived health status increases as the household income and the educational level increases; also as the age decreases, among men and in the richest region of the country (and decreases in the poorest regions).

Table 1. Self-perceived health status according to selected variables. Population residing in urban areas of 5000 inhabitants and more, in Argentina, in the year 2013

		Self-perceived health status		Total
		Excellent or very good	Good, fair or poor	
Household income quintile per consumer unit	1st. quintile	27.3%	72.7%	6901
	2nd. quintile	30.3%	69.7%	6476
	3rd. quintile	34.8%	65.2%	6669
	4th. quintile	40.3%	59.7%	6219
	5th. quintile	48.6%	51.4%	6035
Educational level	Less than elementary school	16.7%	83.3%	3134
	Elementary graduate - secondary undergraduate	27.0%	73.0%	12387
	Secondary graduate - university undergraduate	43.3%	56.7%	11728
	University graduate	52.6%	47.4%	5058
Region of residence	Buenos Aires City	46.1%	53.9%	2853
	Buenos Aires suburban area	30.0%	70.0%	9230
	Pampa	40.6%	59.4%	10821
	Northwest	31.5%	68.5%	3314
	Northeast	28.7%	71.3%	2375
	Cuyo	39.7%	60.3%	2084
	Patagonia	35.5%	64.5%	1689
Gender	Male	38.5%	61.5%	15352
	Female	33.6%	66.4%	17013
Age group	Aged 18 – 24	53.1%	46.9%	5355
	Aged 25 – 34	46.8%	53.2%	7090
	Aged 35 – 49	36.7%	63.3%	8603
	Aged 50 – 64	23.2%	76.8%	6416
	Aged 65 and older	16.6%	83.4%	4903
Total		35.9%	64.1%	32365

Source: Own elaboration based on the ENFR 2013.

In Table 2 we begin by presenting a binary logistic regression in Model I, in which we incorporate all the independent and the dependent variables introduced in Table 1. Given the independent variables have a certain level of correlation, the regression will allow us to observe if -once the effect of the other variables is controlled- each of the variables continues to have an effect on self-perceived health status. For example, the population of Buenos Aires City has higher incomes and educational levels than the residents of other regions. The regression will allow us to answer if -once the effects of educational level and income are controlled- the population living in Buenos Aires City continues to have greater chances of having a very good or excellent self-perceived health status. On the other hand, in Models II, III and IV, we incorporated to Model I the interaction of gender with household income quintile per consumer unit, as well as with educational level and with age group (respectively). The incorporation of these interactions will allow us to find out whether inequalities by income, educational level and age in the self-perceived health status remain constant between men and women, or if they vary significantly by gender. It should be noted that we have also attempted to carry out two other models in which we included the interaction between three variables (including gender, age group and educational level in one of them, and the interaction between gender, age group and household income quintile per consumer unit in the other). The results of these interactions were not statistically significant.

Table 2. Logistic regression: odds ratio of factors that affect very good or excellent self-perceived health status. Population residing in urban areas of 5000 inhabitants and more in Argentina in the year 2013

	Model I	Model II	Model III	Model IV
Household income quintile per consumer unit (1st. quintile reference)	-	-	-	
2nd. Quintile	1,18**	1,42**	1,18**	1,18**
3rd. quintile	1,46**	1,73**	1,46**	1,46**
4th. Quintile	1,62**	1,88**	1,62**	1,61**
5th. Quintile	2,08**	2,43**	2,09**	2,08**
Educational level (Less than elementary school reference)	-	-	-	

Table 2. (Continued)

	Model I	Model II	Model III	Model IV
Elementary graduate - secondary undergraduate	1,18**	1,18**	1,26**	1,18**
Secondary graduate - university undergraduate	1,85**	1,86**	2,08**	1,86**
University graduate	3,12**	3,12**	3,61**	3,13**
Region of residence (Buenos Aires City reference)	-	-	-	
Buenos Aires suburban area	0,61**	0,62**	0,61**	0,61**
Pampa	1,03+	1,03+	1,03+	1,03+
Northwest	0,68**	0,68**	0,68**	0,68**
Northeast	0,59**	0,59**	0,59**	0,59**
Cuyo	0,97+	0,97+	0,96+	0,97+
Patagonia	0,69**	0,69**	0,68**	0,69**
Gender (Female reference)	1,24**	1,64**	1,51**	0,97+
Age group (Aged 65 and older reference)	-	-	-	
Aged 18 – 24	6,67**	6,67**	6,62**	6,00**
Aged 25 – 34	4,24**	4,24**	4,21**	3,81**
Aged 35 – 49	2,70**	2,70**	2,68**	2,32**
Aged 50 – 64	1,38**	1,37**	1,37**	1,24**
1st. quintile of household income per consumer unit and female reference	N/C	-	N/C	N/C
2nd. quintile and male	N/C	0,68**	N/C	N/C
3rd. quintile and male	N/C	0,71**	N/C	N/C
4th. quintile and male	N/C	0,73**	N/C	N/C
5th. quintile and male	N/C	0,73**	N/C	N/C
Less than elementary school and female reference	N/C	N/C	-	N/C
Elementary graduate - secondary undergraduate and male	N/C	N/C	0,88+	N/C
Secondary graduate - university undergraduate and male	N/C	N/C	0,80*	N/C
University graduate and male	N/C	N/C	0,73**	N/C
Aged 65 and older and female reference	N/C	N/C	N/C	
Aged 18 – 24 and male	N/C	N/C	N/C	1,29**
Aged 25 – 34 and male	N/C	N/C	N/C	1,29**
Aged 35 – 49 and male	N/C	N/C	N/C	1,40**
Aged 50 – 64 and male	N/C	N/C	N/C	1,27**
Constant	0,10	0,09	0,09	0,11
Nagelkerke (Pseudo) R^2	0,19	0,19	0,19	0,19

Notes: (1) 0 = Poor, fair or good; 1 = Very good or excellent.
** $p < 0,01$; * $p < 0,05$; + $p > 0,05$, N/C not considered.
Source: Own elaboration based on the ENFR 2013.

In Model I we observe that all independent variables continue to have an effect on self-perceived health status once the rest of the variables are controlled. We observe that those who belong to households in the fifth income quintile have twice as many odds (2.08) of having a very good or excellent self-perceived health status than those in the first quintile. Those who completed higher education have three times (3.12) greater odds of having that very same self-perception of health status than those who reached less than primary education. On the other hand, those who reside in Buenos Aires City have greater odds of having a very good or excellent self-perceived health status than those who reside in the Northeast or Northwest, in Buenos Aires suburban area or in Patagonia; but there are no statistically significant differences with those who reside in Cuyo or in Pampa region. Men are 24% more likely than women to have this positive self-perceived health status, while younger people (aged 18 to 24) have more than six times (6.67) more odds than older adults (aged 65 and older).

In Model II we maintain the same variables as in Model I, but we also incorporate the interaction between the household income quintile and gender. Special attention must be paid to the terms of interaction, when incorporating an interaction into a logistic regression, without disregard for the original variables that are part of the interaction (in this case, household income and gender). As shown in Table 2, the effect of the rest of the variables (educational level, region of residence and age group) is not modified -or its modifications are minimal-. Regarding the original variables, the models now show the effect of each of them for the reference category of the other variable that is part of the interaction (e.g., the income effect on women's self-perceived health status). Regarding income, we see that the differences become deeper between the first quintile and the rest of the quintiles. This is because Model II points out the income effect only for women (reference category for gender in the interaction). We can say then that the women placed in the fifth quintile have 2.43 times more odds of having an excellent or very good self-perceived health status than those in the first quintile (when we considered men and women, in Model I, those odds were 2.08). In turn, now the gender variable shows the effect of being a man only for those who belong to the first income quintile. That is, men in the first income quintile are 1.64 times more likely to have excellent or very good self-rated health than women in the same quintile (in Model I - considering gender differences for all quintiles- that value was 1.24). Finally, we observe that all the terms of the interaction are statistically significant. This means that gender differences in the self-perceived health status are statistically more important in the first income quintile than in quintiles 2, 3, 4 and 5.

In Model III we incorporate the same variables as in Model I and add the interaction between educational level and gender. Once again, the effect of the rest of the variables that are not part of the interaction is not modified. Starting with the terms of the interaction, we observe that gender differences are significantly greater among those who have not completed elementary school than among those who have completed high school (with 95% confidence level) or even higher education (with 99% confidence level). In contrast, there are no significant differences with secondary school undergraduates. When we focus on the educational level and only compare women (Model III) instead of women and men (Model I), we observe that the values of the odds ratios slightly increase for elementary graduates and secondary school undergraduates (it goes from 1.18 in Model I to 1.26 in Model III). These values also went remarkably up for those who have completed secondary school (goes from 1.85 to 2.08) as well as for those who completed higher education (goes from 3.12 to 3.61). That is to say, the differences triggered by the educational level in the self-perceived health status of women, actually increase in Model III, but these differences are more intense in the highest educational levels. On the other hand, we observe that gender differences also grow in comparison with Model I. Now, focusing only on those who have completed less than elementary studies, men have 1.51 times more odds of having a very good or excellent health status than women (in Model I -considering all educational levels- these chances were 1.24 times higher).

Finally, in Model IV we incorporate the interaction between gender and age group. As in Models II and III, the variables that are not part of the interaction have not modified their effect with respect to Model I. Focusing on the terms of the interaction, we observe that gender differences are significantly more important in all age groups compared with the older population (65 and older). In this line, when focusing on the effect of the gender variable, we see that it ceases to be statistically significant. That means, gender differences in the self-perception of health status are not statistically significant in the population aged 65 and older (once the effect of the rest of the variables has been controlled). On the other hand, we observe that the differences due to age decrease in Model IV (which only shows the differences between women) in relation to the effect of Model I (which considers men and women). For example, in Model I, those who belong to the age group of 18 to 24 have 6.67 times more odds of reporting a very good or excellent self-perceived health status than people aged 65 and older; unlike Model IV where those odds are 6.00.

Conclusion

In this chapter, we pointed out the theoretical importance of intersectionality to understand social inequalities in health. At the same time, we outlined the different possible quantitative approaches that we advise (or disadvise) so as to address this topic and we postulated that -in addition to the statistical model- the theoretical interpretation of data is fundamental to develop an intersectional analysis.

Then we moved forward towards the analysis of inequalities in the self-perception of health status in Argentina. We began with a descriptive analysis, observing that those who have higher educational levels, live in higher income households, reside in the highest income regions of the country, who are also younger and of male gender, have a better self-perception of their health status. Then we incorporated the variables in a binary logistic regression. In Model I we observed that each of the independent variables retained a net effect on self-perceived health status once the remaining independent variables were controlled. So far, we had performed an additive type of analysis, which did not consider the intersectionality between different independent variables. Many Argentinean antecedents carried out the same analysis about this topic, and their results share similarities with our results, in the fact that women, older people, and those in lower positions in the social structure (by income, educational level and/or social class) have a worse self-perception of their health status (MSAL 2006, 2011, 2012, 2015; Jorrat et al., 2008; Alazraqui et al., 2009; Adaszko, 2011; Ballesteros, 2014; Observatorio de la Deuda Social Argentina, 2015; Rodríguez Espínola and Filgueira, 2018; Sarti and Rodríguez Espinosa, 2018). As we pointed out, this type of analysis fails to disclose whether there is a differential effect in the combinatorial of the different positions of the subjects. The case of low-educated women actually raises a question, do they add up the disadvantages for being a woman and for having low educational level? Or does the combination of these social positions bring about an effect that actually worsens these two disadvantages? In order to move forward towards this intersectional analysis and to account for the multiplicative nature of social inequalities, we incorporated interactions within the logistic regression models: between gender and household income per consumer unit (Model II), between gender and educational level (Model III) and between gender and age group (Model IV). These models allowed us to observe that gender inequalities are significantly deepened among people living in households with lower economic resources (Model II) and among people with lower educational resources (Model III), but they are less intense among older adults (Model IV).

The collected data, once compared with previous studies about intersectionality between gender and social position, and its impact on the self-perceived health status, showed inconstant results. In a previous work, with the analysis of both a different survey and a different statistical model (differential logistic regressions for men and women) (Krause and Ballesteros 2018), we managed to advance in the study of Argentina. As in this chapter, we found greater gender inequalities in the self-perception of health status of low-income population. However, there are also international studies that found an inverse intersectional relationship; that is an attenuation of gender inequalities among the population with fewer economic resources (Veenstra 2011). In turn, Matthews et al. (1999) found no significant gender differences that stem from the different social classes.

The results based on the educational level relied on the age of the cohort: at the age of 33 there were no significant gender differences, while at age of 23 -in line with what we found out in our analysis- differences by educational level were significantly greater for women than for men.

One of the possible reasons to explain the interaction, in the sense detected here, is that gender relations are more asymmetric in the lower-income population than among those with greater resources (Ariza and De Oliveira 1996, Borrell et al. 2004, Sen et al. 2005, Esteban 2006). The burden of the "double shift" or "triple shift" -of remunerated work, domestic responsibilities and caregiving- seems to be greater for women pertaining to households of lower income quintiles partly because of these sociocultural dispositions but also due to the lack of economic resources to hire help. This can directly affect their health causing stress and worsening their quality of life (García Calvente et al. 2004, Sen et al. 2005, Esteban 2006), but it can also affect their health in an indirect way, due to time shortage to carry out activities which could enhance their health, such as peer socialization activities or recreational physical activity (Frisby et al. 1997, Hargreaves 1993, Hormiga-Sánchez 2015, Ray 2014, Ballesteros et al. 2018).

In turn, the weight of the double or triple shift of feminine work, according to the stage in the family life cycle, could be the reason for fewer gender inequalities between self-perceived health status among older women and men. That is to say, even though older women also suffer the feminization of caregiving (being responsible for the wellbeing of brothers, grandchildren and other family members), this burden could be less demanding than looking after children of school age and living under the same roof (Montaño Virreira 2012). There are studies carried out with older adult population that -in line with our results- have not found significant gender differences in the self-perception of health status (Fernandez-Martinez et al. 2012, Machón et al. 2016). However, there also exist other studies, which found out that men have a better self-perception of health status within this age group (Gonzalo and Paserín 2004, Razzaque et al. 2010).

In short, by applying an intersectional approach to the analysis of health inequities, we followed the international recommendations to no longer understand the population's health as crossed by independent axes of inequality: for example, women's health, educated people's health or low-income sectors' health. On the contrary, the development of intersectionality in the field of population health aims to understand that gender –as well as any other system of inequality- should not be separated from others since these are coproduced at the macrostructural level and they are simultaneously experienced at the microsocial level. In this chapter, we verified that gender inequalities in the self-perception of health status are broadened in sectors with lower economic and educational resources; and are also less significant for the older population. This probably occurs because gender is "created" in different contexts (West and Zimmerman 1987) according to factors linked to many aspects of human life: e.g., the labor market, the distribution of domestic tasks and caregiving work at home, as well as psychosocial factors and cultural stereotypes, etc. These results have allowed us to advance in the knowledge of the complexity of the social inequalities in health in Argentina.

REFERENCES

Adaszko, Dan. (2011). "La salud de la población y el acceso al sistema que la atiende". In *Estado de Situación del Desarrollo Humano y Social: Barreras estructurales y dualidades de la sociedad argentina en primer año del Bicentenario*, edited by Agustín Salvia, 136-176. Buenos Aires: Educa. ["The health of the population and access to the system that attends it". In *Situation Status of Human and Social Development: Structural Barriers and Dualities of Argentine Society in the First Year of the Bicentennial*, edited by Agustín Salvia, 136-176. Buenos Aires: Educa].

Aguilar, Omar., Pérez, Pablo., Ananías, Rubén., Mora, Claudia. & Blanco, Osvaldo. (2016). "The intersection between class and gender and its impact on the quality of employment in Chile". *CEPAL Review, 120*, 131-151.

Alazraqui, Marcio., Diez, Roux., Ana, V., Fleischer., Nancy, y Spinelli, Hugo. (2009). "Salud auto-referida y desigualdades sociales, Ciudad de

Buenos Aires, Argentina, 2005". *Salud Colectiva, 25*(9), 1990–2000. ["Self-referred health and social inequalities, City of Buenos Aires, Argentina, 2005". *Collective Health, 25*(9), 1990-2000].

Ariza, Marina. & De Oliveira, Orlandina. (1996). "Inequidades de género y de clase". In *La condición femenina: una propuesta de indicadores*, edited by Orlandina De Oliveira, Marina Ariza, Marcela Eternod, María de la Paz López, and Vania Salles. México: SOMEDE-CONAPO. ["Inequities of gender and class". In *The female condition: a proposal of indicators*, edited by Orlandina De Oliveira, Marina Ariza, Marcela Eternod, María de la Paz López, and Vania Salles. Mexico: SOMEDE-CONAPO].

Artazcoz, Lucía., Borrell, Carme. & Benach, Joan. (2001). "Gender inequalities in health among workers: the relation with family demands". *J Epidemiol Community Health, 55*(9), 639-647. Accessed February 14, 2019. doi: 10.1136/jech.55.9.639.

Ballesteros, Matías Salvador., Freidin, Betina., Wilner, Agustín. & López Rendina, Lucas. (2018). "Deporte y ejercicio: un análisis interseccional de las desigualdades sociales". Paper presented at the First World Forum of Critical Thinking organized by CLACSO, Buenos Aires, Argentina, November 19- 23. ["Sport and exercise: an intersectional analysis of social inequalities". Paper presented at the First World Forum of Critical Thinking organized by CLACSO, Buenos Aires, Argentina, November 19-23].

Ballesteros, Matías Salvador. (2014). *Un análisis sobre las desigualdades en el acceso a los servicios de salud en Argentina a partir de datos secundarios.* Documentos de Jóvenes Investigadores. Buenos Aires: Instituto de Investigaciones Gino Germani. http://webiigg.sociales.uba.ar/iigg/textos/documentos/dji41.pdf. [*An analysis of inequalities in access to health services in Argentina based on secondary data.* Documents of Young Researchers. Buenos Aires: Gino Germani Research Institute. http: //webiigg.sociales. uba.ar/iigg/textos/ documentos/dji41.pdf].

Ballesteros, Matías Salvador. (2018). "Promedio de los efectos marginales e interacciones en las regresiones logísticas binarias". *INCASI Working*

Paper Series, *3*. ["Average of the marginal effects and interactions in the binary logistic regressions". *INCASI Working Paper Series*, 3].

Bauer, Greta R. & Scheim, Ayden I. (2019). "Methods for analytic intercategorical intersectionality in quantitative research: Discrimination as a mediator of health inequalities". *Social Science & Medicine*, *226*, 236-245. Accessed March 23, 2019. doi: 10.1016/j.socscimed.2018.12.015.

Borrell, Carme. & Artazcoz, Lucía. (2008). "Las desigualdades de género en salud: retos para el futuro". *Revista Española de Salud Pública*, *82*(3), 241-249. ["Gender inequalities in health: challenges for the future". *Spanish Journal of Public Health*, *82*(3), 241-249].

Borrell, Carme., García-Calvente, María del Mar. & Martí-Bosca, José Vicente. (2004). "La salud pública desde la perspectiva de género y clase social". *Gaceta Sanitaria*, *18*(1), 2-6. ["Public health from the perspective of gender and social class". *Sanitary Gazette*, *18*(1), 2-6].

Bowleg, Lisa. (2008). "When Black+ lesbian+ woman≠ Black lesbian woman: The methodological challenges of qualitative and quantitative intersectionality research". *Sex roles*, *59*(5-6), 312-325. Accessed February 14, 2019. doi: 10.1007/s11199-008-9400-z.

Bowleg, Lisa. (2012). "The problem with the phrase women and minorities: intersectionality—an important theoretical framework for public health". *American journal of public health*, *102*(7), 1267-1273. Accessed February 22, 2019. doi: 10.2105/AJPH.2012.300750.

Bowleg, Lisa y Bauer. & Greta, R. (2016). "Invited reflection: Quantifying intersectionality". *Psychology of Women Quarterly*, *40*(3), 337-341. Accessed February 11, 2019. doi: 10.1177/0361684316654282.

Davis, Kathy. (2008). "Intersectionality as buzzword: A sociology of science perspective on what makes a feminist theory successful". *Feminist theory*, *9*(1), 67-85. Accessed February 14, 2019. doi: 10.1177/1464700108086364.

Else-Quest, Nicole M. & Hyde, Janet S. (2016a). "Intersectionality in quantitative psychological research: I. Theoretical and epistemological issues". *Psychology of Women Quarterly*, *40*(2), 155-170. Accessed February 11, 2019. doi: 10.1177/0361684316629797.

Else-Quest, Nicole M. & Hyde, Janet S. (2016b). "Intersectionality in quantitative psychological research: II. Methods and techniques". *Psychology of Women Quarterly*, *40*(3), 319-336. Accessed February 11, 2019. doi: 10.1177/0361684316647953.

Esteban, María Luz. (2006). "Estudio de la salud y el género, las ventajas de un enfoque antropológico y feminista". *Salud colectiva*, *2*(1), 9-20 ["Study of health and gender, the advantages of an anthropological and feminist approach". *Collective health*, *2*(1), 9-20].

Evans, Clare R. (2019). "Adding interactions to models of intersectional health inequalities: Comparing multilevel and conventional methods". *Social Science & Medicine*, *221*, 95-105. Accessed February 14, 2019. doi: 10.1016/j.socscimed.2018.11.036.

Fernández, Martínez., Beatriz, Prieto Flores., María, Eugenia., Forjaz, María João., Fernández, Mayoralas., Gloria, Rojo Pérez. & Fermina, Martínez Martín Pablo. (2012). "Self-perceived health status in older adults: regional and sociodemographic inequalities in Spain". *Rev. Saúde Pública*, *46*(2), 310-319. Accessed March 14, 2019. doi: 10.1590/S0034-89102012000200013.

Frisby, W., Crawford, S. & Dorer, T. (1997). Reflections on Participatory Action Research: The Case of Low-Income Women Accessing Local Physical Activity services. *Journal of Sport Management.*, *11*(1), 8-28. Accessed March 25, 2019. doi: 10.1123/jsm.11.1.8.

García, Calvente María del Mar., Jiménez, Rodrigo., María, Luis. & Martínez, Morante, Emilia. (2010). *Guía para incorporar la perspectiva de género a la investigación en salud*. Granada: Escuela Andaluza de Salud Pública. https://www.repositoriosalud.es/bitstream/ 10668/2575/3/Garcia_GuiaIncorporarPerspectiva.pdf. [*Guide to incorporate the gender perspective in health research.* Granada: Andalusian School of Public Health. https://www.repositoriosalud. es/bitstream/ 10668/2575/3 / Garcia_GuiaIncorporarPerspectiva.pdf.]

García, Calvente., María, del Mar., Mateo Rodríguez, Inmaculada. & Maroto Navarro, Gracia. (2004). "El impacto de cuidar en la salud y la calidad de vida de las mujeres". *Gaceta Sanitaria*, *18*(5), 83-92. ["The impact of taking care of health and women's quality of life". *Sanitary Gazette, 18*(5), 83-92].

Gonzalo, Elena. & Paserín, María Isabel. (2004). "La salud de las personas mayores". *Gaceta Sanitaria, 18*(1), 69-80. ["The health of the elderly". *Sanitary Gazette, 18*(1), 69-80].

Hargreaves, Jennifer. (1993). "Promesa y problemas en el ocio y los deportes femeninos". In *Materiales de sociología del deporte*, edited by Jean Marie Brohm, Pierre Bourdieu, Eric Dunning, Jennifer Hargreaves, Terry Todd, and Keving Young, 109-132. Madrid: Ediciones La Piqueta. ["Promise and problems in leisure and women's sports". In *Sports sociology materials*, edited by Jean Marie Brohm, Pierre Bourdieu, Eric Dunning, Jennifer Hargreaves, Terry Todd, and Keving Young, 109-132. Madrid: Ediciones La Piqueta].

Hormiga Sánchez, Claudia Milena. (2015). "Perspectiva de género en el estudio de la práctica de actividad física". *Rev Cienc Salud, 13*(2), 233-48. Accessed March 21, 2019. doi: dx.doi.org/10.12804/revsalud13.02.2015.08. ["Perspective of gender in the study of the practice of physical activity". *Health Sciences Review, 13*(2), 233-48. Accessed March 21, 2019. doi: dx.doi.org/10.12804/revsalud13.02.2015.08].

Jorrat, Raúl Fernández., María, de las Mercedes. & Marconi, Elida H. (2008). "Utilización y gasto en servicios de salud de los individuos en Argentina en 2005. Comparaciones internacionales de diferenciales socioeconómicos en salud". *Salud Colectiva, 4*(1), 57–96. ["Use and expenditure on health services of individuals in Argentina in 2005. International comparisons of socioeconomic differentials in health". *Collective Health, 4*(1), 57-96.

Krause, Mercedes. & Ballesteros, Matías Salvador. (2018). "Interseccionalidad en desigualdades en salud en Argentina: discusiones teórico-metodológicas a partir de una encuesta poblacional". *Revista Hacia la Promoción de la Salud, 23*(2), 13-33. Accessed February 15, 2019. doi: 10.17151/ hpsal.2018.23.2.2. ["Intersectionality in health inequalities in Argentina: theoretical-methodological discussions based on a population survey". *Towards the Promotion of Health Review,*

23(2), 13-33. Accessed February 15, 2019. doi: 10.17151 / hpsal.2018.23.2.2].

López, Elsa., Findling, Liliana. & Abramzón, Mónica. (2006). "Desigualdades en Salud: ¿Es Diferente la Percepción de Morbilidad de Varones y Mujeres?". *Salud Colectiva, 2*(1), 61-67. ["Inequalities in Health: Is the Perception of Morbility of Men and Women Different?". *Collective Health, 2*(1), 61-67].

Machón, Mónica., Vergara, Itziar., Dorronsoro, Miren., Vrotsou, Kalliopi. & Larrañaga, Isabel. (2016). "Self-perceived health in functionally independent older people: associated factors". *BMC geriatrics, 16*(66), 1-9. Accessed March 25, 2019. doi: 10.1186/s12877-016-0239-9.

Marecek, Jeanne. (2016). "Invited reflection: Intersectionality theory and feminist psychology". *Psychology of Women Quarterly, 40*(2), 177-181. Accessed February 12, 2019. doi: 10.1177/0361684316641090.

Matthews, Sharon., Manor, Orly. & Power, Chris. (1999). "Social inequalities in health: are there gender differences?". *Social science & medicine, 48*(1), 49-60. Accessed February 15, 2019. doi: 10.1016/ S0277-9536(98)00288-3.

McCall, Leslie. (2005). "The complexity of intersectionality". In *Intersectionality and Beyond* edited by Emily Grabham, Davida Cooper, Jane Krishnadas, and Didi Herman, 65-92. Oxon: Routledge-Cavendish.

Montaño Virreira, S. (2012). "Las mujeres mayores y el envejecimiento con dignidad en América Latina". In *Los derechos de las personas mayores en el siglo XXI: situación, experiencias y desafíos* edited by Sandra Huenchuan, 311-324. México: CEPAL/Gobierno de la Ciudad de México. ["Older women and aging with dignity in Latin America". In *The rights of the elderly in the 21st century: situation, experiences and challenges* edited by Sandra Huenchuan, 311-324. Mexico: CEPAL/Government of Mexico City].

MSAL. (2006). *Encuesta Nacional de Factores de Riesgo 2005 Versión Completa*. Buenos Aires: Ministerio Salud de la Nación. [National Survey of Risk Factors 2005 Full Version. Buenos Aires: National Ministry of Health in Argentina].

MSAL. (2011). *Segunda encuesta nacional de factores de riesgo para enfermedades no transmisibles*. Buenos Aires: Ministerio Salud de la Nación. http://www.msal.gob.ar/images/stories/bes/graficos/ 00000005 70cnt-2014-10_encuesta-nacional-factores-riesgo-2011_informe-final.pdf. [*Second National Survey of Risk Factors for non-communicable diseases*. Buenos Aires: National Ministry of Health in Argentina. http://www.msal.gob.ar/images/stories/bes/graficos/ 00000005 70cnt-2014-10_encuesta-nacional-factores-riesgo-2011_ informe-final.pdf].

MSAL. (2012). *Encuesta de utilización y gasto en servicios de salud. Argentina- Año 2010. Primeros resultados*. Buenos Aires: Ministerio de Salud de la Nación. [*Survey of utilization and expenditure in health services. Argentina- Year 2010. First results*. Buenos Aires: National Ministry of Health in Argentina].

MSAL. (2015). *Tercera Encuesta Nacional de Factores de Riesgo para enfermedades no transmisibles*. Buenos Aires: Ministerio de Salud de la Nación. http://www.msal.gob.ar/images/stories/bes/ graficos/ 0000000544cnt-2015_09_04_encuesta_nacional_factores_riesgo.pdf. [*Third National Survey of Risk Factors for non-communicable diseases*. Buenos Aires: National Ministry of Health in Argentina. http://www.msal.gob.ar/images/stories/bes/ graficos/ 0000000544cnt-2015_09_04_encuesta_nacional_factores_riesgo.pdf].

Observatorio de la Deuda Social Argentina. (2015). *Salud percibida: cobertura, utilización y acceso al sistema de atención de la salud en el área metropolitana de Buenos Aires*. Buenos Aires: Educa. http://wadmin.uca.edu.ar/public/ckeditor/Salud_Percibida_3_Sept.pdf [*Perceived health: coverage, use and access to the health care system in the metropolitan area of Buenos Aires*. Buenos Aires: Educa. http://wadmin.uca.edu.ar/public/ckeditor/Salud_Percibida_3_Sept.pdf].

Ocampo, José Mauricio. (2010). "Self-rated health: Importance of use in elderly adults". *Colombia Médica*, *41*(3), 275-289.

Ray, Rashawn. (2014). "An Intersectional Analysis to Explaining a Lack of Physical Activity Among Middle Class Black Women". *Sociology*

Compass, *8*(6), 780–91. Accessed February 27, 2019. doi: 10.1111/soc4.12172.

Razzaque, Abdur., Nahar, Lutfun., Khanam, Masuma Akter. & Streatfield, Peter Kim. (2010). "Socio-demographic differentials of adult health indicators in Matlab, Bangladesh: self-rated health, health state, quality of life and disability level". *Global Health Action*, *3*(1), 70-77. Accessed February 14, 2019. doi: 10.3402/gha.v3i0.4618.

Richman, Laura. S. & Zucker, Alyssa N. (2019). "Quantifying intersectionality: An important advancement for health inequality research". *Social Science & Medicine*, *226*, 246-248. Accessed February 21, 2019. doi: 10.1016/j.socscimed.2019.01.036.

Rodríguez Espínola, Solange. & Filgueira, Pilar. (2018). *La salud de las mujeres urbanas en edad fértiles*. Buenos Aires: Educa. [*The health of urban women of childbearing age*. Buenos Aires: Educa].

Rohlfs, Izabella., Borrell, Carme. & Fonseca, M. do C. "Género, desigualdades y salud pública: conocimientos y desconocimientos". *Gac Sanit*, *14*(3), 60-71. ["Gender, inequalities and public health: knowledge and ignorance". *Sanitary Gazette*, *14*(3), 60-71].

Sarti, Simone. & Rodríguez Espinola, Solange. (2018). "Health inequalities in Argentina and Italy: A comparative analysis of the relation between socio-economic and perceived health conditions". *Research in Social Stratification and Mobility*, *55*, 89–98. Accessed February 21, 2019. doi: 10.1016/j.rssm.2018.04.004.

Sen, Gita., George, Asha. & Östlin, Piroska. (2005). *Incorporar la perspectiva de género en la equidad en salud: un análisis de la investigación y las políticas*. Whashington: Organización Panamericana de la Salud. [*To incorporate the gender perspective in health equity: an analysis of research and policies*. Washington: Pan American Health Organization].

Seng, Julia S., Lopez, William D., Sperlich, Mickey., Hamama, Lydia. & Meldrum, Caroline D. R. (2012). "Marginalized identities, discrimination burden, and mental health: Empirical exploration of an interpersonal-level approach to modeling intersectionality". *Social*

Science & Medicine, 75(12), 2437-2445. Accessed February 2, 2019. doi:10.1016/j.socscimed.2012.09.023.

Veenstra, Gerry. (2011). "Race, gender, class, and sexual orientation: intersecting axes of inequality and self-rated health in Canada". *International journal for equity in health*, *10*(1), 3. Accessed February 7, 2019. doi: 10.1186/1475-9276-10-3.

Warner, Leah R. (2016). "Invited reflection: Contested interpretations and methodological choices in quantitative research". *Psychology of Women Quarterly*, *40*(3), 342-346. Accessed February 11, 2019. doi: 10.1177/0361684316655453.

Warner, Leah R., Settles, Isis H. & Shields, Stephanie A. (2016). "Invited reflection: Intersectionality as an epistemological challenge to psychology". *Psychology of Women Quarterly*, *40*(2), 171-176. Accessed February 11, 2019. doi: 10.1177/0361684316641384.

West, Candace. & Zimmerman, Don H. (1987). "Doing gender". *Gender & society*, *1*(2), 125-151. Accessed February 24, 2019. doi: 10.1177/0891243287001002002.

BIBLIOGRAPHY

A village goes mobile: telephony, mediation, and social change in rural India

LCCN	2018031662
Type of material	Book
Personal name	Tenhunen, Sirpa, author.
Main title	A village goes mobile: telephony, mediation, and social change in rural India / Sirpa Tenhunen.
Published/Produced	New York, NY: Oxford University Press, [2018]
Description	1 online resource.
ISBN	9780190630294 (updf)
	9780190630300 (epub)
	9780190876562 (online course)
LC classification	HE9715.I4
Summary	"This book examines how mobile telephony contributes to social change in rural India on the basis of ethnographic fieldwork. The book investigates how the use of mobile phones has influenced economic, political and social relationships including gender relationships, and how these new social constellations relate to

	culture and development" -- Provided by publisher.
Contents	Theorizing phone use contexts and mediation -- Why mobile phones became ubiquitous: remediation and socialities -- Mobile telephony, economy and social logistics -- Mediating gender: mobile phones and women's agency -- Mediating conflict: mobile telephony and politics -- Smartphones, caste and intersectionalities.
Subjects	Cell phones--Social aspects--India.
	Cell phones--Economic aspects--India.
	Telecommunication--Economic aspects--India.
	Cell phone services industry--India.
	Intersectionality (Sociology)--India.
	India--Rural conditions.
Notes	Includes bibliographical references and index.
Additional formats	Print version: Tenhunen, Sirpa, author. Village goes mobile New York, NY: Oxford University Press, [2018] 9780190630270 (DLC) 2017041847
Series	Studies in mobile communication

A village goes mobile: telephony, mediation, and social change in rural India

LCCN	2017041847
Type of material	Book
Personal name	Tenhunen, Sirpa, author.
Main title	A village goes mobile: telephony, mediation, and social change in rural India / Sirpa Tenhunen.
Published/Produced	New York, NY: Oxford University Press, [2018]
Description	ix, 200 pages: illustrations; 24 cm.
ISBN	9780190630270 (cloth: alk. paper)
	9780190630287 (pbk.: alk. paper)
LC classification	HE9715.I4 T46 2018

Summary	"This book examines how mobile telephony contributes to social change in rural India on the basis of ethnographic fieldwork. The book investigates how the use of mobile phones has influenced economic, political and social relationships including gender relationships, and how these new social constellations relate to culture and development" -- Provided by publisher.
Contents	Theorizing phone use contexts and mediation -- Why mobile phones became ubiquitous: remediation and socialities -- Mobile telephony, economy and social logistics -- Mediating gender: mobile phones and women's agency -- Mediating conflict: mobile telephony and politics -- Smartphones, caste and intersectionalities.
Subjects	Cell phones--Social aspects--India.
	Cell phones--Economic aspects--India.
	Telecommunication--Economic aspects--India.
	Cell phone services industry--India.
	Intersectionality (Sociology)--India.
	India--Rural conditions.
Notes	Includes bibliographical references and index.
Additional formats	Online version: Tenhunen, Sirpa, author. Village goes mobile New York, NY: Oxford University Press, [2018] 9780190630294 (DLC) 2018031662
Series	Studies in mobile communication

Audacious voices: profiles in intersectional feminism

LCCN	2018947565
Type of material	Book
Personal name	Blake, Holly J. (Jacklyn) author.

Main title	Audacious voices: profiles in intersectional feminism / Holly J. Blake and Melissa D. Ooten.
Published/Produced	Berkeley, CA: She Writes Press, [2018] ©2018
Description	xiv, 172 pages; 22 cm
ISBN	9781631524912 1631524917
LC classification	HM488.5 .B535 2018
Related names	Ooten, Melissa, author.
Summary	Inspiring and hopeful, Audacious Voices is a collection of twelve stories from alumnae/alumni of WILL*, a feminist model for education. Each author featured in this book is working, in their own distinct way, to make their communities more equitable-and their stories illustrate how different elements of the WILL* program influence and inspire them to act with such intentionality. Author-activist Courtney Martin writes in The New Better Off that the times we live in may break our hearts, but they don't have to break our spirit; it's that spirit that these stories capture, alongside the power of a feminist educational program that engenders such spirit. Emphasizing hope, empathy, resiliency, and solutions by showcasing the transformative power of inclusive leadership, advocacy, and mentorship, Audacious Voices reminds us that real change is possible, even in the current political climate.
Subjects	Feminism. Intersectionality (Sociology) Feminism. Intersectionality (Sociology)
Notes	Includes bibliographical references.

Black feminism reimagined: after intersectionality

LCCN	2018034093
Type of material	Book
Personal name	Nash, Jennifer C., 1980- author.
Main title	Black feminism reimagined: after intersectionality / Jennifer C. Nash.
Published/Produced	Durham: Duke University Press, 2019.
Description	1 online resource.
ISBN	9781478002253 (ebook)
LC classification	HQ1197
Contents	A love letter from a critic, or notes on the intersectionality wars -- The politics of reading -- Surrender -- Love in the time of death -- Coda: Some of us are tired.
Subjects	Womanism--United States.
	Feminism--United States.
	Intersectionality (Sociology)
	Feminist theory.
	Women's studies--United States.
	Universities and colleges--United States--Sociological aspects.
Notes	Includes bibliographical references and index.
Additional formats	Print version: Nash, Jennifer C., 1980- author. Black feminism reimagined Durham: Duke University Press, 2019 9781478000433 (DLC) 2018026166
Series	Next wave

Black feminism reimagined: after intersectionality

LCCN	2018026166
Type of material	Book
Personal name	Nash, Jennifer C., 1980- author.
Main title	Black feminism reimagined: after intersectionality / Jennifer C. Nash.

Published/Produced	Durham: Duke University Press, 2019.
Description	xi, 170 pages; 23 cm.
ISBN	9781478000433 (hardcover: alk. paper)
	9781478000594 (pbk.: alk. paper)
LC classification	HQ1197 .N37 2019
Contents	A love letter from a critic, or notes on the intersectionality wars -- The politics of reading -- Surrender -- Love in the time of death -- Coda: Some of us are tired.
Subjects	Womanism--United States.
	Feminism--United States.
	Intersectionality (Sociology)
	Feminist theory.
	Women's studies--United States.
	Universities and colleges--United States--Sociological aspects.
Notes	Includes bibliographical references and index.
Additional formats	Online version: Nash, Jennifer C., 1980- author. Black feminism reimagined Durham: Duke University Press, 2019 9781478002253 (DLC) 2018034093
Series	Next wave new directions in women's studies
	Next wave.

Distortion: social processes beyond the structured and systemic

LCCN	2017040533
Type of material	Book
Main title	Distortion: social processes beyond the structured and systemic / edited by Nigel Rapport.
Published/Produced	Abingdon, Oxon; New York, NY: Routledge, 2018.
Description	1 online resource.
ISBN	9781315317540 (E-book)
LC classification	HM488.5

Related names	Rapport, Nigel, 1956- editor.
Contents	Conceptualizing the distortion of human social life / Nigel Rapport -- Contorted environments and distorted being / Henrik Vigh -- A blind man's problem: distortion and non-responsiveness; or, The construction of non-futures in Danish bureaucracy / Nina Holm Vohnsen -- Distortion and Stanley Spencer's life in art / Nigel Rapport -- The politics of paradox: Kierkegaardian theology and national conservatism in Denmark / Morten Axel Pedersen -- Into the "crack": Scottish agricultural revolutions and the art of moaning / Morten Nielsen -- Chains of distortion: resistance and relationality in the creation of new ideas in a Danish innovation agency / Lise Røjskjær Pedersen -- "Hello, can you hear me better now?": mediatized acoustemologies and distortion on the radio / Sandra Lori Petersen -- Epi-pro-logue: an anthropological theory of distortion / Morten Nielsen and Morten Axel Pedersen.
Subjects	Intersectionality (Sociology)
	Intersectionality (Sociology)--Case studies.
Notes	Includes bibliographical references and index.
Additional formats	Print version: Distortion Abingdon, Oxon; New York, NY: Routledge, 2018 9781138230651 (DLC) 2017032945
Series	Routledge studies in anthropology

Distortion: social processes beyond the structured and systemic

LCCN	2017032945
Type of material	Book
Main title	Distortion: social processes beyond the structured and systemic / edited by Nigel Rapport.

Bibliography

Published/Produced	Abingdon, Oxon; New York, NY: Routledge, 2018.
ISBN	9781138230651 (hardback: alk. paper)
LC classification	HM488.5 .D57 2018
Related names	Rapport, Nigel, 1956- editor.
Contents	Conceptualizing the distortion of human social life / Nigel Rapport -- Contorted environments and distorted being / Henrik Vigh -- A blind man's problem: distortion and non-responsiveness; or, The construction of non-futures in Danish bureaucracy / Nina Holm Vohnsen -- Distortion and Stanley Spencer's life in art / Nigel Rapport -- The politics of paradox: Kierkegaardian theology and national conservatism in Denmark / Morten Axel Pedersen -- Into the "crack": Scottish agricultural revolutions and the art of moaning / Morten Nielsen -- Chains of distortion: resistance and relationality in the creation of new ideas in a Danish innovation agency / Lise Røjskjær Pedersen -- "Hello, can you hear me better now?": mediatized acoustemologies and distortion on the radio / Sandra Lori Petersen -- Epi-pro-logue: an anthropological theory of distortion / Morten Nielsen and Morten Axel Pedersen.
Subjects	Intersectionality (Sociology)
	Intersectionality (Sociology)--Case studies.
Notes	Includes bibliographical references and index.
Additional formats	Online version: Distortion Abingdon, Oxon; New York, NY: Routledge, 2018 9781315317540 (DLC) 2017040533
Series	Routledge studies in anthropology

Excluded within: the (un)intelligibility of radical political actors

LCCN	2017011887

Type of material	Book
Personal name	Kramer, Sina.
Main title	Excluded within: the (un)intelligibility of radical political actors / Sina Kramer.
Published/Produced	New York, NY: Oxford University Press, [2017]
Description	xii, 241 pages; 25 cm
ISBN	9780190625986 (hardcover: alk. paper)
LC classification	JC575 .K73 2017
Subjects	Equality.
	Political rights.
	Political science--Philosophy.
	Marginality, Social.
	Intersectionality (Sociology)
	Political participation--Case studies.
	Social action--Case studies.
	Social movements--Case studies.
Notes	Includes bibliographical references (pages [193]-229) and index.

For the love of men: a new vision for mindful masculinity

LCCN	2019016751
Type of material	Book
Personal name	Plank, Liz, author.
Main title	For the love of men: a new vision for mindful masculinity / Liz Plank.
Edition	First edition.
Published/Produced	New York: ST. Martin's Press, [2019]
ISBN	9781250196248 (hardcover)
LC classification	BF692.5 .P59 2019
Subjects	Masculinity.
	Men--Social aspects.
	Intersectionality (Sociology)
Notes	Includes bibliographical references.

Gender and class in contemporary South Korea: intersectionality and transnationality

LCCN	2019002949
Type of material	Book
Main title	Gender and class in contemporary South Korea: intersectionality and transnationality / edited by Hae Yeon Choo, John Lie, and Laura C.Nelson.
Published/Produced	Berkeley: Institute of East Asian Studies, University of California, Berkeley, [2019]
Description	1 online resource.
ISBN	9781557291837 ()
	1557291837 ()
LC classification	HQ18.K6
Related names	Choo, Hae Yeon, editor.
	Lie, John, editor.
	Nelson, Laura C., editor.
Summary	"The contributors to this volume offer an explicitly intersectional and transnational perspective on contemporary South Korean gender and class relations and structures"-- Provided by publisher.
Contents	Introduction: gender, class, and contemporary South Korea / Hae Yeon Choo, John Lie, Laura C.Nelson -- Changelings and cinderellas: class in/equality, gendered social im/mobility, and post-developmentalism in contemporary South Korean -- Television dramas / Jin-kyung Lee -- Shrewd entrepreneurs or immoral speculators?: desires, speculation, and middle-class housewives in South Korea, 1978-1996 / Myungji Yang -- "My skill": attachments and narratives of garment workers in South Korea / Seo Young Park -- Leave no birthing trace: the politics of health and beauty in the South Korean postpartum care

	market / Yoonjung Kang -- Gendered narratives of transition to adulthood among Korean work-bound youth / Hyejeong Jo -- Diverging masculinities and the politics of aversion toward ethnically mixed men in the Korean military / Hyun Mee Kim -- Maternal guardians: intimate labor and the pursuit of gendered citizenship among South Korean volunteers helping migrant women / Hae Yeon Choo.
Subjects	Sex--Korea (South)
	Social classes--Korea (South)
	Intersectionality (Sociology)--Korea (South)
Notes	Includes bibliographical references.
Additional formats	Print version: Gender and class in contemporary South Korea Berkeley: Institute of East Asian Studies, University of California, Berkeley, [2019] 9781557291820 (DLC) 2018057410
Series	Transnational Korea; 4

Gender and class in contemporary South Korea: intersectionality and transnationality

LCCN	2018057410
Type of material	Book
Main title	Gender and class in contemporary South Korea: intersectionality and transnationality / edited by Hae Yeon Choo, John Lie, and Laura C. Nelson.
Published/Produced	Berkeley: Institute of East Asian Studies, University of California, Berkeley, [2019]
Description	viii,169 pages; 23 cm.
ISBN	9781557291820 (alk. paper)
	1557291829 (alk. paper)
LC classification	HQ18.K6 G46 2019
Related names	Choo, Hae Yeon, editor.
	Lie, John, editor.

Summary	Nelson, Laura C., editor. "The contributors to this volume offer an explicitly intersectional and transnational perspective on contemporary South Korean gender and class relations and structures"-- Provided by publisher.
Subjects	Sex--Korea (South) Social classes--Korea (South) Intersectionality (Sociology)--Korea (South)
Notes	Includes bibliographical references.
Additional formats	Online version: Gender and class in contemporary South Korea Berkeley: Institute of East Asian Studies, University of California, Berkeley, [2019] 9781557291837 (DLC) 2019002949
Series	Transnational Korea; 4

Gender and the abjection of Blackness

LCCN	2017037080
Type of material	Book
Personal name	Bröck-Sallah, Sabine, 1954- author.
Main title	Gender and the abjection of Blackness / Sabine Broeck.
Published/Produced	Albany, NY: SUNY Press, 2018.
Description	viii, 230 pages; 24 cm.
ISBN	9781438470399 (hardcover: alk. paper)
LC classification	HQ1201 .B83 2018
Contents	Against gender. Enslavism and the subjects of feminism -- Abolish property: Black feminist struggles against anti-Blackness -- Gender and the grammar of enslavism -- Abjective returns: the slave's fungibility in white gender studies -- Post gender, post human: Braidotti 's Nietzschean echoes of anti-blackness -- On dispossession as a false analogy.

Subjects	Women, Black.
	Blacks--Race identity.
	Racism.
	Womanism.
	Feminism.
	Intersectionality (Sociology)
	Slavery.
Notes	Includes bibliographical references and index.
Series	SUNY series in gender theory

Gender, intersections, and institutions: intersectional groups building alliances and gaining voice in Germany

LCCN	2017018832
Type of material	Book
Main title	Gender, intersections, and institutions: intersectional groups building alliances and gaining voice in Germany / edited by Louise K. Davidson-Schmich.
Published/Produced	Ann Arbor: University of Michigan Press, 2017.
Description	xii, 284 pages; 25 cm
ISBN	9780472130535 (hardcover: alk. paper)
LC classification	JN3971.A38 M545 2017
Related names	Davidson-Schmich, Louise K., 1968- editor.
Subjects	Minorities--Political activity--Germany.
	Minorities--Civil rights--Germany.
	Pressure groups--Germany.
	Intersectionality (Sociology)--Political aspects--Germany.
	Germany--Politics and government--1990-
Notes	Includes bibliographical references and index.

Hollywood at the intersection of race and identity

LCCN	2019007367
Type of material	Book

Main title	Hollywood at the intersection of race and identity / edited by Delia Malia Caparoso Konzett.
Published/Produced	New Brunswick: Rutgers University Press, [2019]
ISBN	9780813599311 (pbk.)
LC classification	PN1995.9.I34 H65 2019
Related names	Konzett, Delia Caparoso, editor of compilation.
Subjects	Identity (Psychology) in motion pictures.
	Race in motion pictures.
	Motion pictures--United States--History.
	Intersectionality (Sociology)--United States.
Notes	Includes bibliographical references and index.

Intersectional care for black boys in an alternative school: they really care about us

LCCN	2018059714
Type of material	Book
Personal name	Ransom, Julia C., author.
Main title	Intersectional care for black boys in an alternative school: they really care about us / Julia C. Ransom.
Published/Produced	Lanham, Maryland: Lexington Books, [2019]
Description	1 online resource.
ISBN	9781498551311 (electronic)
LC classification	LC2771
Summary	"This book explores the possibilities that exist within educational spaces for Black male students when teachers care for these students while also acknowledging the intersectionality of Black male identity and the potential oppression and resilience that they experience as the result"-- Provided by author.
Contents	On black boys and the importance of care -- The ethic of care -- Authentic vs. aesthetic care -- Culturally responsive pedagogy and caring --

Critical caring -- Care through intersectionality -- Vulnerable and disconnected with a story to tell -- The barriers black boys face in schooling -- About the study -- Study locale: midcoast city -- The school site -- Educational context at achieveed -- The students and their teacher -- College and career readiness class -- About the researcher -- Uncaring spaces and places -- Absence of care: past high school experiences -- Personal and social battles -- Conflicts and turmoil -- Disengaged, disregarded, and invisible -- Finding a new path -- The intersectionality of care for young black men -- Intersectionality and being a young black man in the school and the city -- Approaches to identity -- Neutral stance or rejection of stereotypes?: a unique case -- Identity, privilege, and oppression in the classroom -- Identity, privilege, and oppression permeable borders -- Intersectional identities, care, and student-teacher relationships -- Intersectional care and feeling the love -- Acknowledging the intersections of self and students -- The ethic of care and authentic care through care-based education strategies -- Cultural, social, and political positionality: culturally responsive practices -- The presence of care: feeling the love with intersectional care -- Conclusion: the implications of intersectionality and care for black males -- The theoretical and practical notion of intersectional care -- Black boys, opportunity gaps, and equitable education -- Reflections on care for black boys, and girls.

Subjects   African American boys--Education--Social aspects.

	Alternative schools--United States.
	Intersectionality (Sociology)--United States.
	Racism in education--United States.
	African Americans--Race identity.
Notes	Includes bibliographical references and index.
Additional formats	Print version: Ransom, Julia C., author. Intersectional care for black boys in an alternative school Lanham, Maryland: Lexington Books, [2019] 9781498551304 (DLC) 2018048501
Series	Race and education in the twenty-first century

Intersectional care for Black boys in an alternative school: they really care about us

LCCN	2018048501
Type of material	Book
Personal name	Ransom, Julia C., author.
Main title	Intersectional care for Black boys in an alternative school: they really care about us / Julia C. Ransom.
Published/Produced	Lanham, Maryland: Lexington Books, [2019]
Description	xx, 138 pages; 24 cm.
ISBN	9781498551304 (cloth: alk. paper)
LC classification	LC2771 .R36 2019
Summary	"This book explores the possibilities that exist within educational spaces for Black male students when teachers care for these students while also acknowledging the intersectionality of Black male identity and the potential oppression and resilience that they experience as the result"-- Provided by author.
Contents	On black boys and the importance of care -- The ethic of care -- Authentic vs. aesthetic care -- Culturally responsive pedagogy and caring -- Critical caring -- Care through intersectionality --

Bibliography

Vulnerable and disconnected with a story to tell -- The barriers black boys face in schooling -- About the study -- Study locale: midcoast city -- The school site -- Educational context at achieveed -- The students and their teacher -- College and career readiness class -- About the researcher -- Uncaring spaces and places -- Absence of care: past high school experiences -- Personal and social battles -- Conflicts and turmoil -- Disengaged, disregarded, and invisible -- Finding a new path -- The intersectionality of care for young black men -- Intersectionality and being a young black man in the school and the city -- Approaches to identity -- Neutral stance or rejection of stereotypes?: a unique case -- Identity, privilege, and oppression in the classroom -- Identity, privilege, and oppression permeable borders -- Intersectional identities, care, and student-teacher relationships -- Intersectional care and feeling the love -- Acknowledging the intersections of self and students -- The ethic of care and authentic care through care-based education strategies -- Cultural, social, and political positionality: culturally responsive practices -- The presence of care: feeling the love with intersectional care -- Conclusion: the implications of intersectionality and care for black males -- The theoretical and practical notion of intersectional care -- Black boys, opportunity gaps, and equitable education -- Reflections on care for black boys, and girls.

Subjects African American boys--Education--Social aspects.
Alternative schools--United States.

	Intersectionality (Sociology)--United States.
	Racism in education--United States.
	African Americans--Race identity.
Notes	Includes bibliographical references (page 111-130) and index.
Additional formats	Online version: Ransom, Julia C., author. Intersectional care for black boys in an alternative school Lanham, Maryland: Lexington Books, [2019] 9781498551311 (DLC) 2018059714
Series	Race and education in the twenty-first century

Intersectional theology: an introductory guide

LCCN	2018276252
Type of material	Book
Personal name	Kim, Grace Ji-Sun, 1969- author.
Main title	Intersectional theology: an introductory guide / Grace Ji-Sun Kim and Susan M. Shaw.
Published/Produced	Minneapolis, MN: Fortress Press, [2018] ©2018
Description	xix, 129 pages; 23 cm
ISBN	1506446094 (pbk.: alk. paper)
	9781506446097 (pbk.: alk. paper)
Related names	Shaw, Susan M. (Susan Maxine), 1960- author.
Summary	Intersectional Theology: An Introductory Guide offers a new approach to theology that encourages centering of social differences and structures of power in the ways we think about God, the church, and other theological categories. Rooted in intersectionality, a tool of analysis developed primarily by black feminists, intersectional theology calls for examination of theological ideas from multifaceted and ever-changing perspectives that move us toward social justice.

Contents	Introduction to intersectionality -- Biography as intersectional theology -- Intersectionality as theological method -- Applying intersectionality to theology and the Bible -- Practicing intersectional theology -- Conclusion.
Subjects	Intersectionality (Sociology)
	Social justice.
	Christian sociology.
	Theology--Methodology.
	Christian sociology.
	Intersectionality (Sociology)
	Social justice.
	Theology--Methodology.
Notes	Includes bibliographical references (pages 119-122) and index.

Intersectionality and higher education: identity and inequality on college campuses

LCCN	2018038053
Type of material	Book
Main title	Intersectionality and higher education: identity and inequality on college campuses / edited by W. Carson Byrd, Rachelle J. Brunn-Bevel, and Sarah M. Ovink.
Published/Produced	New Brunswick: Rutgers University Press, [2019]
Description	vii, 295 pages; 24 cm
ISBN	9780813597669 (pbk.)
	9780813597676 (cloth)
LC classification	LC212.42 .I57 2019
Related names	Byrd, W. Carson, editor.
	Brunn-Bevel, Rachelle J., editor.
	Ovink, Sarah M., editor.
Summary	"Though colleges and universities are arguably paying more attention to diversity and inclusion

Contents

than ever before, to what extent do their efforts result in more socially just campuses? This book examines how race, ethnicity, class, gender, sexuality, sexual orientation, age, disability, nationality, and other identities connect to produce intersected campus experiences"-- Provided by publisher.

Always crossing boundaries, always existing in multiple bubbles: intersected experiences and positions on college campuses / Rachelle J. Brunn-Bevel, Sarah M. Ovink, W. Carson Byrd, and Antron D. Mahoney -- The contingent climate: exploring student perspectives at a racially diverse institution / Marcela G. Cuellar and R. Nicole Johnson-Ahorlu -- More than immigration status: undocumented students in U.S. Jesuit higher education / Terry-Ann Jones -- Race-based assumptions of social class identity and their consequences at a predominantly white (and wealthy) institution / Deborah M. Warnock -- Biracial college students' racial identity work: how black-white biracial students navigate racism and privilege at historically black and historically white institutions / Kristen A. Clayton -- The still furious passage of the black graduate student / Victor E. Ray -- Faculty members from low socioeconomic status backgrounds: student mentorship, motivations, and intersections / Elizabeth M. Lee and Tonya Maynard -- Doing less with less: faculty care work in times of precarity / Denise Goerisch -- Faculty assessments as tools of oppression: a black woman's reflections on colorblind racism in the academy / Bedelia N. Richards -- "Diversity" goals and faculty of color: supporting racial inclusion and awareness in general-education courses / Melanie Jones Gast, Ervin (Maliq) Matthew, and Derrick R. Brooms -- Pursuing intersectionality as a pedagogical tool in the higher education classroom / Orkideh Mohajeri, Fernando Rodriguez, and Finn Schneider -- Intersecting identities and student affairs professionals / Ophelie Rowe-Allen and Meredith Smith -- Studying STEM while black: how institutional agents prepare black students for the racial realities of stem environments / Tonisha B. Lane -- Exclusion, perspective taking, and the liminal role of higher education staff in supporting students with disabilities / Annemarie Vaccaro and Ezekiel Kimball -- Making room for gendered possibilities: using intersectionality to discover transnormative inequalities in the women's college admissions process / Megan Nanney -- Troubling diversity: an intersectional analysis of diversity action plans at U.S. flagship universities / Susan V. Iverson -- Tips of icebergs in the ocean: reflections on future research for embracing intersectionality in higher education / W. Carson Byrd, Sarah M. Ovink, and Rachelle J. Brunn-Bevel.

Subjects Discrimination in higher education--United States.
Racism in higher education--United States.
Educational equalization--United States.
Minorities--Education (Higher)--United States.
Intersectionality (Sociology)
Identity (Psychology)

Notes Includes bibliographical references and index.

Intersectionality and identity politics

LCCN	2018023075
Type of material	Book
Main title	Intersectionality and identity politics / M.M. Eboch, book editor.
Published/Produced	New York: Greenhaven Publishing, [2019]
ISBN	9781534504240 (library bound)
	9781534504851 (pbk.)
LC classification	HM488.5 .I584 2019
Related names	Eboch, M. M., editor.
Contents	What's the point of intersectionality and identity politics? -- Will intersectionality unite or divide people? -- Where should we go with identity politics? -- For further reading -- Index -- Picture credits.
Subjects	Intersectionality (Sociology)--United States.
	Identity politics--United States.
Notes	Includes bibliographical references and index. Grades 7-12.
Series	Introducing issues with opposing viewpoints

Intersectionality as critical social theory

LCCN	2018061091
Type of material	Book
Personal name	Hill Collins, Patricia, author.
Main title	Intersectionality as critical social theory / Patricia Hill Collins.
Published/Produced	Durham: Duke University Press, 2019.
ISBN	9781478005421 (hardcover: alk. paper)
	9781478006466 (pbk.: alk. paper)
LC classification	HM488.5 .H56 2019
Contents	Intersectionality as critical inquiry -- What's critical about critical social theory? -- Intersectionality and resistant knowledge projects

	-- Who gets to tell intersectionality's story? -- Intersectionality, experience and community -- Intersectionality and the question of freedom -- Violence, relationality and intersecting power relations -- Intersectionality without social justice?
Subjects	Intersectionality (Sociology)
	Critical theory.
	Social change.
	Social justice.
Notes	Includes bibliographical references and index.
Additional formats	Online version: Hill Collins, Patricia, author. Intersectionality as critical social theory Durham: Duke University Press, 2019 9781478007098 (DLC) 2019005395

Intersectionality as critical social theory

LCCN	2019005395
Type of material	Book
Personal name	Hill Collins, Patricia, author.
Main title	Intersectionality as critical social theory / Patricia Hill Collins.
Published/Produced	Durham: Duke University Press, 2019.
Description	1 online resource.
ISBN	9781478007098 (ebook)
LC classification	HM488.5
Contents	Intersectionality as critical inquiry -- What's critical about critical social theory? -- Intersectionality and resistant knowledge projects -- Who gets to tell intersectionality's story? -- Intersectionality, experience and community -- Intersectionality and the question of freedom -- Violence, relationality and intersecting power

	relations -- Intersectionality without social justice?
Subjects	Intersectionality (Sociology)
	Critical theory.
	Social change.
	Social justice.
Notes	Includes bibliographical references and index.
Additional formats	Print version: Hill Collins, Patricia, author. Intersectionality as critical social theory Durham: Duke University Press, 2019 9781478005421 (DLC) 2018061091

Intersectionality of race, ethnicity, class, and gender in teaching and teacher education: movement toward equity in education

LCCN	2018021399
Type of material	Book
Main title	Intersectionality of race, ethnicity, class, and gender in teaching and teacher education: movement toward equity in education / Edited by Norvella P. Carter and Michael Vavrus.
Published/Produced	Leiden; Boston: Brill Sense, [2018]
Description	1 online resource.
ISBN	9789004365209 (E-book)
LC classification	LC1099.515.C85
Related names	Carter, Norvella P., editor.
	Vavrus, Michael J., editor.
Summary	"In Intersectionality of Race, Ethnicity, Class, and Gender in Teaching and Teacher Education, the editors bring together scholarship that employs an intersectionality methodology to conditions that affect public school children, teachers, and teacher educators. Chapter authors use intersectionality to examine group identities not only for their differences and experiences of

oppression, but also for differences within groups that contribute to conflicts among groups. This collection moves beyond single-dimension conceptions that undermines legal thinking, disciplinary knowledge, and social justice. Intersectionality in this collection helps complicate static notions of race, ethnicity, class, and gender in education. Hence, this book stands as an addition to research on educational equity in relation to institutional systems of power and privilege" -- Provided by publisher.

Contents

Introduction: intersectionality related to race, ethnicity, class and gender / Norvella P. Carter -- Intersectionality, colonizing education, and the Indigenous voice of survivance / John P. Hopkins -- Intersectional considerations for teaching diversity / China M. Jenkins -- Intersections of race and class in preservice teacher education: advancing educational equity / Kamala V. Williams and Quinita Ogletree -- The elephant in the room: approaches of white educators to issues of race and racism / Amy J. Samuels -- Teaching African American and Latinx learners: moving beyond a status quo punitive disciplinary context to considerations for equitable pedagogy in teacher education / Gwendolyn C. Webb-Hasan, Victoria L. Jones and Chi Yun Moon -- Intersectionality of ethnicity, gender, and disability with disciplinary practices used with Indigenous students: Implications for teacher preparation and development / Denise K. Whitford -- "That kind of affection ain't welcome from a black man": the intersections of race and gender in the elementary classroom" / Dawn

Tafari -- We're not misbehaving: cultivating the spirit of defiance in black male students / Marlon C. James, Kelly Ferguson, Willie C. Harmon Jr. and Kevin L. Jones -- Black girls matter: an intersectional analysis of young black women's experiences and resistance to dominating forces in school / Julia Daniel and Terrenda White -- Latinx and education: shattering stereotypes / Monica Vasquez Neshyba -- Intersecting histories in the present: deconstructing how white preservice teachers at rural South African schools perceive their black supervising teacher and students / Warren Chalklen -- Epilogue: movement toward a "third reconstruction" and educational equity / Michael Vavrus.

Subjects   Culturally relevant pedagogy.
Intersectionality (Sociology)
Educational equalization.
Teachers--Training of--Social aspects.

Notes   Includes bibliographical references and index.

Additional formats   Print version: Intersectionality of race, ethnicity, class, and gender in teaching and teacher education Leiden; Boston: Brill Sense, [2018] 9789004365186 (DLC) 2018007395

Series   Advances in teaching and teacher education; 3

Intersectionality of race, ethnicity, class, and gender in teaching and teacher education: movement toward equity in education

LCCN   2018007395
Type of material   Book
Main title   Intersectionality of race, ethnicity, class, and gender in teaching and teacher education: movement toward equity in education / Edited by

Norvella P. Carter and Michael Vavrus, foreword by Geneva Gay.

Published/Produced Leiden; Boston: Brill Sense, [2018]
Description xvii, 181 pages; 23 cm.
ISBN 9789004365186 (pbk.: alk. paper)
9789004365193 (hardback: alk. paper)
LC classification LC1099.515.C85 I67 2018
Related names Carter, Norvella P., editor.
Vavrus, Michael J., editor.
Summary "In Intersectionality of Race, Ethnicity, Class, and Gender in Teaching and Teacher Education, the editors bring together scholarship that employs an intersectionality methodology to conditions that affect public school children, teachers, and teacher educators. Chapter authors use intersectionality to examine group identities not only for their differences and experiences of oppression, but also for differences within groups that contribute to conflicts among groups. This collection moves beyond single-dimension conceptions that undermines legal thinking, disciplinary knowledge, and social justice. Intersectionality in this collection helps complicate static notions of race, ethnicity, class, and gender in education. Hence, this book stands as an addition to research on educational equity in relation to institutional systems of power and privilege" -- Provided by publisher.
Contents Introduction: intersectionality related to race, ethnicity, class and gender / Norvella P. Carter -- Intersectionality, colonizing education, and the Indigenous voice of survivance / John P. Hopkins -- Intersectional considerations for teaching diversity / China M. Jenkins -- Intersections of

race and class in preservice teacher education: advancing educational equity / Kamala V. Williams and Quinita Ogletree -- The elephant in the room: approaches of white educators to issues of race and racism / Amy J. Samuels -- Teaching African American and Latinx learners: moving beyond a status quo punitive disciplinary context to considerations for equitable pedagogy in teacher education / Gwendolyn C. Webb-Hasan, Victoria L. Jones and Chi Yun Moon -- Intersectionality of ethnicity, gender, and disability with disciplinary practices used with Indigenous students: Implications for teacher preparation and development / Denise K. Whitford -- "That kind of affection ain't welcome from a black man": the intersections of race and gender in the elementary classroom" / Dawn Tafari -- We're not misbehaving: cultivating the spirit of defiance in black male students / Marlon C. James, Kelly Ferguson, Willie C. Harmon Jr. and Kevin L. Jones -- Black girls matter: an intersectional analysis of young black women's experiences and resistance to dominating forces in school / Julia Daniel and Terrenda White -- Latinx and education: shattering stereotypes / Monica Vasquez Neshyba -- Intersecting histories in the present: deconstructing how white preservice teachers at rural South African schools perceive their black supervising teacher and students / Warren Chalklen -- Epilogue: movement toward a "third reconstruction" and educational equity / Michael Vavrus.

Subjects   Culturally relevant pedagogy.
Intersectionality (Sociology)

Bibliography

	Educational equalization.
	Teachers--Training of--Social aspects.
Notes	Includes bibliographical references (pages 173-178) and index.
Additional formats	Online version: Intersectionality of race, ethnicity, class, and gender in teaching and teacher education Leiden; Boston: Brill Sense, [2018] 9789004365209 (DLC) 2018021399
Series	Advances in teaching and teacher education; 3

Introducing intersectionality

LCCN	2017013088
Type of material	Book
Personal name	Romero, Mary, author.
Main title	Introducing intersectionality / Mary Romero.
Published/Produced	Cambridge; Medford, MA: Polity Press, 2018
Description	viii, 212 pages; 23 cm.
ISBN	9780745663661 (hardback)
	9780745663678 (pbk.)
LC classification	HM488.5 .R65 2018
Contents	Introduction -- Identifying intersectionality -- Where does intersectionality come from? -- Intersectionality in everyday campus life -- Intersectionality and social identities: examining gender -- Exploring interlocking systems of oppression and privilege -- Intersectional approaches to social issues: the wealth gap, the care crisis, and black lives matter -- Conclusion: intersectionality and social justice.
Subjects	Intersectionality (Sociology)
Notes	Includes bibliographical references (pages 174-195) and index.
Additional formats	Online version: Romero, Mary, author. Introducing intersectionality Malden, MA: Polity

	Press, [2017] 9781509525287 (DLC) 2017035338
Series	Short introductions

Just research: widening the methodological imagination in contentious times

LCCN	2018000136
Type of material	Book
Personal name	Fine, Michelle, author.
Main title	Just research: widening the methodological imagination in contentious times / Michelle Fine.
Published/Produced	New York, NY: Published by Teachers College Press, [2018] ©2018
Description	1 online resource.
ISBN	9780807776681 (ebook)
LC classification	HM480
Contents	Loss and desire: bearing witness in white working class suburban New Jersey -- Family his/her-stories -- Tracing the biography of our research questions -- Commitments of critical research -- Circling back -- Exiles within -- Wild tongues and critical bifocals at the radical margins -- Critical bifocality: situating lives in historical and structural analysis -- Exiled from school: re-framing dropouts -- Exiled from home: when Muslim-American youth learned they didn't belong -- Critical bifocality as theory-method -- Civics lessons -- The color and class of educational betrayal and desire / with April Burns, Maria Elena Torre, and Yasser A. Payne -- Learning from those who endure: the dynamics of focus groups -- Cumulative inequity: schooling toward alienation -- Hearing problems: a violation

Bibliography

of procedural justice -- College going, perhaps -- Civics lessons -- "Wicked problems", "Flying monkeys" and prec(ar)ious lives: a matter of time? / with A. Cory Greene and Sonia Sanchez -- Curating testimony -- The cumulative weight of growing up in precarity -- Building schools for educational, racial and labor justice -- Just methods: historic and contemporary laboratories of critical knowledge production -- The veins of critical participatory action research -- The public science project -- Echoes of brown: documenting the unfulfilled promise of educational integration -- Do you believe in Geneva? Critical par with the global human rights campaign -- Critical PAR: kneading, translating, and braiding across and within -- "Speaking words of wisdom": -- Metabolizing oppression into radical wit and activism / with Maria Elena Torre, David Frost, and Allison Cabana -- Coloniality of being -- Queer youth under siege: what's your issue? -- "Willful subjects": no research on us without us -- Conclusion: critical participatory research and democracy: igniting the slow fuse of the research imagination -- Whose science? Whose evidence? -- Critical participatory research: a provisional response-ability toward human freedom and democratic inquiry.

Subjects Critical theory--Methodology.
Intersectionality (Sociology)
Interdisciplinary approach to knowledge.
Marginality, Social.

Notes Includes bibliographical references and index.

Additional formats Print version: Fine, Michelle, author. Just research New York, NY: Published by Teachers College

Press, [2018] 9780807758748 (DLC) 2017039601

Just research in contentious times: widening the methodological imagination

LCCN	2017039601
Type of material	Book
Personal name	Fine, Michelle, author.
Main title	Just research in contentious times: widening the methodological imagination / Michelle Fine.
Published/Produced	New York: Teachers College Press, [2018] ©2018
Description	xvi, 144 pages: illustrations; 23 cm
ISBN	9780807758748 (hardcover: alk. paper) 9780807758731 (pbk.: alk. paper)
LC classification	HM480 .F48 2018
Contents	Loss and desire: bearing witness in white working class suburban New Jersey -- Family his/her-stories -- Tracing the biography of our research questions -- Commitments of critical research -- Circling back -- Exiles within -- Wild tongues and critical bifocals at the radical margins -- Critical bifocality: situating lives in historical and structural analysis -- Exiled from school: re-framing dropouts -- Exiled from home: when Muslim-American youth learned they didn't belong -- Critical bifocality as theory-method -- Civics lessons -- The color and class of educational betrayal and desire / with April Burns, Maria Elena Torre, and Yasser A. Payne -- Learning from those who endure: the dynamics of focus groups -- Cumulative inequity: schooling toward alienation -- Hearing problems: a violation of procedural justice -- College going, perhaps --

Civics lessons -- "Wicked problems", "Flying monkeys" and prec(ar)ious lives: a matter of time? / with A. Cory Greene and Sonia Sanchez -- Curating testimony -- The cumulative weight of growing up in precarity -- Building schools for educational, racial and labor justice -- Just methods: historic and contemporary laboratories of critical knowledge production -- The veins of critical participatory action research -- The public science project -- Echoes of brown: documenting the unfulfilled promise of educational integration -- Do you believe in Geneva? Critical par with the global human rights campaign -- Critical PAR: kneading, translating, and braiding across and within -- "Speaking words of wisdom": -- Metabolizing oppression into radical wit and activism / with Maria Elena Torre, David Frost, and Allison Cabana -- Coloniality of being -- Queer youth under siege: what's your issue? -- "Willful subjects": no research on us without us -- Conclusion: critical participatory research and democracy: igniting the slow fuse of the research imagination -- Whose science? Whose evidence? -- Critical participatory research: a provisional response-ability toward human freedom and democratic inquiry.

Subjects Critical theory--Methodology.
Intersectionality (Sociology)
Interdisciplinary approach to knowledge.
Marginality, Social.

Notes Includes bibliographical references and index.

Additional formats Online version: Fine, Michelle, author. Just research New York, NY: Published by Teachers

College Press, [2018] 9780807776681 (DLC) 2018000136

Mothering while black: boundaries and burdens of middle-class parenthood

LCCN	2018042495
Type of material	Book
Personal name	Dow, Dawn Marie, author.
Main title	Mothering while black: boundaries and burdens of middle-class parenthood / Dawn Marie Dow.
Published/Produced	Oakland, California: University of California Press, [2019]
	©2019
Description	1 online resource.
ISBN	9780520971776 (ebook)
LC classification	HQ759
Summary	"Informed by news stories, such as those of the fatal shootings of Oscar Grant and Trayvon Martin, and engaged with ongoing popular and academic discussions of work and family conflict, Mothering While Black makes significant contributions to the sociology of work and family, race and ethnicity, and gender and culture. Using the analytical lens of intersectionality, it demonstrates that the frameworks typically deployed in research on middle-class mothers and their families, which usually focus on the experiences of elite white mothers, do not adequately capture the experiences of African American middle-class and upper-middle-class mothers. Through sixty in-depth semistructured interviews with African American middle-class and upper-middle-class women, Mothering While Black distills the experiences of these

contemporary mothers, revealing the cultural expectations and constraints that inform their approaches to parenting, work and family, and childcare. Through their accounts, this book demonstrates how race, class, and gender complicate their parenting concerns and strategies, and identifies three aspects of African American middle-class identity that study participants worked to foster in their children. Through this research, the book expands on and revises theories related to parenting, racial identity formation, and family and work conflict by complicating existing frameworks for understanding the cultural pushes and pulls that influence mothers' decision-making"--Provided by publisher.

Contents Introduction: not part of that white mother society -- Creating racial safety and comfort -- Border crossers: understanding struggle -- Border policers: finding our kind of people -- Border transcenders: challenging traditional notions of racial authenticity -- The market-family matrix: the social construction of integrated and conflicted frameworks of work/life balance -- Racial histories of family and work: paid employment is a mother's duty -- Alternative configuration of childrearing: supporting mothers' public sphere activities through extended family parenting -- Conclusion and implications: navigating race, class, and gender in motherhood, parenting and work.

Subjects African American mothers--Social conditions.
Parenting--Social aspects.

	Middle class African Americans--Family relationships.
	Intersectionality (Sociology)
Notes	Includes bibliographical references and index.
Additional formats	Print version: Dow, Dawn Marie, author. Mothering while black Oakland, California: University of California Press, [2019] 9780520300316 (DLC) 2018039768

Mothering while black: boundaries and burdens of middle-class parenthood

LCCN	2018039768
Type of material	Book
Personal name	Dow, Dawn Marie, author.
Main title	Mothering while black: boundaries and burdens of middle-class parenthood / Dawn Marie Dow.
Published/Produced	Oakland, California: University of California Press, [2019] ©2019
ISBN	9780520300316 (cloth: alk. paper) 9780520300323 (paperback)
LC classification	HQ759 .D685 2019
Summary	"Informed by news stories, such as those of the fatal shootings of Oscar Grant and Trayvon Martin, and engaged with ongoing popular and academic discussions of work and family conflict, Mothering While Black makes significant contributions to the sociology of work and family, race and ethnicity, and gender and culture. Using the analytical lens of intersectionality, it demonstrates that the frameworks typically deployed in research on middle-class mothers and their families, which usually focus on the experiences of elite white mothers, do not

Bibliography

adequately capture the experiences of African American middle-class and upper-middle-class mothers. Through sixty in-depth semistructured interviews with African American middle-class and upper-middle-class women, Mothering While Black distills the experiences of these contemporary mothers, revealing the cultural expectations and constraints that inform their approaches to parenting, work and family, and childcare. Through their accounts, this book demonstrates how race, class, and gender complicate their parenting concerns and strategies, and identifies three aspects of African American middle-class identity that study participants worked to foster in their children. Through this research, the book expands on and revises theories related to parenting, racial identity formation, and family and work conflict by complicating existing frameworks for understanding the cultural pushes and pulls that influence mothers' decision-making"--Provided by publisher.

Contents Introduction: not part of that white mother society -- Creating racial safety and comfort -- Border crossers: understanding struggle -- Border policers: finding our kind of people -- Border transcenders: challenging traditional notions of racial authenticity -- The market-family matrix: the social construction of integrated and conflicted frameworks of work/life balance -- Racial histories of family and work: paid employment is a mother's duty -- Alternative configuration of childrearing: supporting mothers' public sphere activities through extended family

	parenting -- Conclusion and implications: navigating race, class, and gender in motherhood, parenting and work.
Subjects	African American mothers--Social conditions.
	Parenting--Social aspects.
	Middle class African Americans--Family relationships.
	Intersectionality (Sociology)
Notes	Includes bibliographical references and index.
Additional formats	Online version: Dow, Dawn Marie, author. Mothering while black Oakland, California: University of California Press, [2019] 9780520971776 (DLC) 2018042495

Muslim women and white femininity: reenactment and resistance

LCCN	2018007974
Type of material	Book
Personal name	Al-Ghabra, Haneen Shafeeq, 1981- author.
Main title	Muslim women and white femininity: reenactment and resistance / Haneen Shafeeq Al-Ghabra.
Published/Produced	New York: Peter Lang, 2018.
Description	x, 193 pages; 23 cm
ISBN	9781433152153 (hardback: alk. paper)
	9781433152160 (pbk.: alk. paper)
	(EBook PDF)
	(ePub)
	(mobi)
LC classification	HQ1170 .A5495 2018
Summary	Muslim Women and White Femininity is a much-needed book at a time where Muslim women are speaking out but also embodying White femininity. This book focuses on how Whiteness travels through Muslim women's bodies who in

turn reenact or resist White womanhood. Through three archetypes: The Oppressed, The Advocate, and the Humanitarian Leader, the author aims to demonstrate the necessity of archetypal criticism as a method that can teach the reader or student how to deconstruct dominant discourses in the media. This book aims to address intercultural, gender, intersectional and critical communication courses but is also suited for the general public who wishes to understand the deceptive nature of the media. Thus, at a time where Muslim women are being used as media objects by Western media, this book is crucial in breaking down how readers can begin to uncover dominant ideologies that are carried through and by Muslim women.

Contents

Understanding the postcolonial and performance through whiteness and intersectionality -- Weaving intersectionality through narrative criticism: western feminism and the marginalization of third world women -- Malala Yousafazai: the oppressed Muslim woman and the search for agency -- Ayaan Hirsi Ali: the advocate and the rejection of Islam -- Queen Rania: the humanitarian leader and the search for a counter-narrative -- Conclusion: the search for an intersectional feminist ethic.

Subjects

Yousafzai, Malala, 1997-
Hirsi Ali, Ayaan, 1969-
Rania, Queen, consort of Abdullah II, King of Jordan, 1970-
Muslim women.
Muslim women--In mass media.
Femininity.
Feminism.

Feminist ethics.
Whites--Race identity.
Intersectionality (Sociology)

Navigating intersectionality: how race, class, and gender overlap

LCCN	2018020654
Type of material	Book
Personal name	Osman, Jamila, author.
Main title	Navigating intersectionality: how race, class, and gender overlap / Jamila Osman.
Published/Produced	New York, NY: Enslow Publishing, [2019]
ISBN	9781978504653 (library bound)
	9781978505605 (pbk.)
LC classification	HM488.5 .O86 2019
Contents	Identity and intersectionality -- Understanding race -- Understanding gender -- Understanding class -- Many struggles, one movement -- Practicing solidarity -- Chapter notes -- Glossary -- Further reading -- Index.
Subjects	Intersectionality (Sociology)
	Group identity.
Notes	Includes bibliographical references and index. Grade 7-12.
Series	Racial literacy

On intersectionality: essential writings

LCCN	2018039330
Type of material	Book
Personal name	Crenshaw, Kimberlé, author.
Main title	On intersectionality: essential writings / Kimberlé Crenshaw.
Published/Produced	New York: New Press, [2019]
ISBN	9781620972700 (pbk.: alk. paper)
LC classification	HM488.5 .C74 2019

Bibliography 121

Subjects	Intersectionality (Sociology)
	Feminist theory.
	Sexism.
	Racism.
Notes	Includes bibliographical references.

Pushing the margins: women of color and intersectionality in LIS

LCCN	2018027564
Type of material	Book
Main title	Pushing the margins: women of color and intersectionality in LIS / Rose L. Chou and Annie Pho, editors.
Published/Produced	Sacramento, CA: Library Juice Press, 2018.
Description	xix, 488 pages; 23 cm.
ISBN	9781634000529 (pbk.: alk. paper)
LC classification	Z682.4.M56 P87 2018
Related names	Chou, Rose L., editor.
	Pho, Annie, editor.
Summary	"Explores the experiences of women of color in library and information science (LIS), using intersectionality as a framework"-- Provided by publisher.
Contents	"When I enter": black women and disruption of the white, heteronormative narrative of librarianship / Caitlin M. J. Pollock and Shelly P. Haley -- Sisters of the stacks / Alexsandra Mitchell -- I am a Muslim, a woman, a librarian: Muslim women and public libraries / Negeen Aghassibake -- The other Asian: reflections of South Asian Americans in libraryland / Nisha Mody, Lalitha Nataraj, Gayatri Singh, and Aditi Worcester -- I am my hair, and my hair is me: #blackgirlmagic in LIS / Teresa Y. Neely -- The voice of a black woman in libraryland: a

theoretical narrative / LaVerne Gray -- A woman of color's work is never done: intersectionality, emotional, and invisible labor in reference and information work / Kawanna Bright -- "Sister, you've been on my mind": experiences of women of color in the library and information sciences profession / Alyse Minter and Genevia M. Chamblee-Smith -- Small brown faces in large white spaces / Rosalinda Hernandez Linares and Sojourna J. Cunningham -- I, too: unmasking emotional labor of women of color community college librarians / Alyssa Jocson Porter, Sharon Spence-Wilcox, and Kimberly Tate-Malone -- The burden of care: cultural taxation of women of color librarians on the tenure-track / Tarida Anantachai and Camille Chesley -- Authenticity vs. professionalism: being true to ourselves at work / Jennifer Brown and Sofia Leung -- Identity, activism, self-care, and women of color librarians / Alanna Aiko Moore and Jan E. Estrellado -- When will my reflection show?: women of color in the Kennesaw State University archives / JoyEllen Freeman -- Selection and self-identity / Robin Bradford and Stephanie Sendaula -- Reflections on the intersection of publishing and librarianship: the experiences of women of color / Charlotte Roh -- Positionality, epistemology, and new paradigms for LIS: a critical dialog with Clara M. Chu / Todd Honma and Clara M. Chu.

Subjects   Minority women librarians--United States.
Minorities in library science--United States.
Women in library science--United States.
Intersectionality (Sociology)

Notes	Includes bibliographical references and index.
Series	Series on critical race studies and multiculturalism in LIS; no. 3

Rac(e)ing to class: confronting poverty and race in schools and classrooms

LCCN	2014953102
Type of material	Book
Personal name	Milner, H. Richard, IV. author.
Main title	Rac(e)ing to class: confronting poverty and race in schools and classrooms / H. Richard Milner IV.
Published/Produced	Cambridge, MA: Harvard Education Press, [2015]
Description	xvi, 212 pages; 24 cm
ISBN	9781612507866 (pbk.)
	9781612507873 (library edition)
LC classification	LC212.2 .M55 2015
Subjects	Racism in education--United States.
	Discrimination in education--United States.
	Educational equalization--United States.
	Intersectionality (Sociology)--United States.
Notes	Includes bibliographical references (pages 187-202) and index.

Racism as zoological witchcraft: a guide for getting out

LCCN	2019014095
Type of material	Book
Personal name	Ko, Aph, author.
Main title	Racism as zoological witchcraft: a guide for getting out / Aph Ko.
Published/Produced	Brooklyn: Lantern Books, [2019]
ISBN	9781590565964 (paperback)
	(ebook other)
LC classification	HT1521 .K54 2019

Summary "In this book, Aph Ko examines the mainstream animal rights and anti-racist movements in an effort to explain why tension exists between the two. She offers possible resolutions, and explores how such tensions represent a symptom of a deeper societal problem. Framed as a "starter guide" for having conversations on race and animals, Racism as Zoological Witchcraft draws upon television shows and films such as Jordan Peele's Get Out, Netflix's Santa Clarita Diet, and ABC's The Bachelor franchise to demonstrate how one can use media and cultural studies to provide new ways of thinking about complex social phenomena. Drawing upon Claire Jean Kim's zoological race theory and James W. Perkinson's European race discourse as witchcraft scholarship, Racism as Zoological Witchcraft concludes that white supremacy functions as a form of zoological witchcraft, a pervasive force that thrives off of metabolizing nonhuman souls. In re-framing white supremacy as a consumptive, cannibalistic force, only then can we re-imagine how Black bodies and animal bodies are used as vehicles to fulfill the racialized power fantasies of the dominant class. This book poses a crucial question: What is the interplay between the ideological and economic consumption of Blackness (both historical and contemporary) and the conception of animals as consumable entities in American society? In Racism as Zoological Witchcraft, Aph Ko argues that in order to "get out" of a problematic system, we have to thoroughly understand how we got in"-- Provided by publisher.

Subjects	Racism--Philosophy.
	Intersectionality (Sociology)
	Feminist theory.
	Veganism--Philosophy.
Additional formats	Online version: Ko, Aph, Racism as zoological witchcraft Brooklyn: 2019. 9781590565971 (DLC) 2019980316

Reclaiming our space: how black feminists are changing the world from the tweets to the streets

LCCN	2018053391
Type of material	Book
Personal name	Jones, Feminista, 1979- author.
Main title	Reclaiming our space: how black feminists are changing the world from the tweets to the streets / Feminista Jones.
Published/Produced	Boston: Beacon Press, 2019.
Description	1 online resource.
ISBN	9780807055380 (ebook)
LC classification	HQ1197
Summary	"A treatise of Black women's transformative influence in media, entertainment, and politics, and why this intersectional movement building, especially on Twitter, is essential to the resistance In Reclaiming Our Space, social worker, activist, and cultural commentator Feminista Jones explores how Black women are changing culture, society, and the landscape of feminism by building digital communities and using social media as powerful platforms. Complex conversations around race, class, and gender that have been happening behind the closed doors of academia for decades are now becoming part of the wider cultural vernacular--one pithy tweet at a

time. These online platforms have given those outside the traditional university setting an opportunity to engage with and advance these conversations--and in doing so have created new energy for intersectional movements around the world. It has been a seismic shift, and as Jones argues, no one has had more to do with this renaissance of community building than Black women. As Jones reveals, some of the best-loved devices of our shared social media language are a result of Black women's innovations, from well-known movement-building hashtags (#BlackLivesMatter, #SayHerName, and #BlackGirlMagic) to the now ubiquitous use of threaded tweets as a marketing and storytelling tool. For some, these online dialogues provide an introduction to the work of Black feminist icons like Angela Davis, Barbara Smith, bell hooks, and the women of the Combahee River Collective. For others, this discourse provides a platform for continuing their feminist activism and scholarship in a new interactive way. With these important online conversations, not only are Black women influencing popular culture and creating sociopolitical movements; they are also galvanizing a new generation to learn and engage in Black feminist thought and theory, and inspiring change in communities around them. Hard-hitting, intelligent, incisive, yet bursting with humor and pop-culture savvy, Reclaiming Our Space is a survey of Black feminism's past, present, and future, and places Black women front and center in a new chapter of resistance and political engagement"-- Provided by publisher.

	"45 years ago, Black American feminists convened as architects for a new revolution that thrives today, finding its home and building its strengths within Black women's online communities and digital spaces"-- Provided by publisher.
Subjects	Womanism--United States.
	Intersectionality--United States.
	Online social networks--United States.
	Social Science / Ethnic Studies / African American Studies.
	Social Science / Feminism & Feminist Theory.
	Social Science / Media Studies.
Notes	Includes bibliographical references.
Additional formats	Print version: Jones, Feminista, 1979- author. Reclaiming our space Boston: Beacon Press, 2019 9780807055373 (DLC) 2018038259

Reclaiming our space: how black feminists are changing the world from the tweets to the streets

LCCN	2018038259
Type of material	Book
Personal name	Jones, Feminista, 1979- author.
Main title	Reclaiming our space: how black feminists are changing the world from the tweets to the streets / Feminista Jones.
Published/Produced	Boston: Beacon Press, 2019.
Description	186 pages; 23 cm
ISBN	9780807055373 (paperback)
LC classification	HQ1197 .J66 2019
Summary	"A treatise of Black women's transformative influence in media, entertainment, and politics, and why this intersectional movement building, especially on Twitter, is essential to the resistance

In *Reclaiming Our Space*, social worker, activist, and cultural commentator Feminista Jones explores how Black women are changing culture, society, and the landscape of feminism by building digital communities and using social media as powerful platforms. Complex conversations around race, class, and gender that have been happening behind the closed doors of academia for decades are now becoming part of the wider cultural vernacular--one pithy tweet at a time. These online platforms have given those outside the traditional university setting an opportunity to engage with and advance these conversations--and in doing so have created new energy for intersectional movements around the world. It has been a seismic shift, and as Jones argues, no one has had more to do with this renaissance of community building than Black women. As Jones reveals, some of the best-loved devices of our shared social media language are a result of Black women's innovations, from well-known movement-building hashtags (#BlackLivesMatter, #SayHerName, and #BlackGirlMagic) to the now ubiquitous use of threaded tweets as a marketing and storytelling tool. For some, these online dialogues provide an introduction to the work of Black feminist icons like Angela Davis, Barbara Smith, bell hooks, and the women of the Combahee River Collective. For others, this discourse provides a platform for continuing their feminist activism and scholarship in a new interactive way. With these important online conversations, not only are Black women influencing popular culture and creating

	sociopolitical movements; they are also galvanizing a new generation to learn and engage in Black feminist thought and theory, and inspiring change in communities around them. Hard-hitting, intelligent, incisive, yet bursting with humor and pop-culture savvy, Reclaiming Our Space is a survey of Black feminism's past, present, and future, and places Black women front and center in a new chapter of resistance and political engagement"-- Provided by publisher.
	"45 years ago, Black American feminists convened as architects for a new revolution that thrives today, finding its home and building its strengths within Black women's online communities and digital spaces"-- Provided by publisher.
Subjects	Womanism--United States.
	Intersectionality--United States.
	Online social networks--United States.
	Social Science / Ethnic Studies / African American Studies.
	Social Science / Feminism & Feminist Theory.
	Social Science / Media Studies.
Notes	Includes bibliographical references.
Additional formats	Online version: Jones, Feminista, 1979- author. Reclaiming our space Boston: Beacon Press, 2019 9780807055380 (DLC) 2018053391

The matrix of race: social construction, intersectionality, and inequality

LCCN	2017032571
Type of material	Book
Personal name	Coates, Rodney D., author.

Main title	The matrix of race: social construction, intersectionality, and inequality / Rodney D. Coates, Miami University of Ohio, Abby L. Ferber, University of Colorado, Colorado Springs, David L. Brunsma, Virginia Tech.
Edition	First Edition.
Published/Produced	Los Angeles: SAGE Publications, [2018]
Description	xvi, 456 pages: illustrations (some color); 24 cm
ISBN	9781452202693 (pbk.: alk. paper)
LC classification	HT1521 .C63 2018
Related names	Brunsma, David L., author.
	Ferber, Abby L., 1966- author.
Contents	Race and social construction of difference -- The shaping of a nation: constructing race in america -- The social construction and regulation of families -- Work and wealth inequality -- Health and healthcare -- Education -- Crime, law and deviance -- Power, politics, and identities -- Sports and the American dream -- Military, war, and terrorism -- References.
Subjects	Race.
	Social constructionism.
	Intersectionality (Sociology)
	Equality.
	United States--Race relations.
Notes	Includes index.

The Queer Intersectional in contemporary Germany: essays on racism, capitalism and sexual politics

LCCN	2018448327
Type of material	Book
Main title	The Queer Intersectional in contemporary Germany: essays on racism, capitalism and sexual politics / Christopher Sweetapple (ed.); with

	contributions by Judith Butler [and 6 others]; translated from the German by Yossi Bartal [and 3 others].
Edition	First English edition.
Published/Produced	Giessen: Psychosozial-Verlag, 2018.
Description	208 pages; 21 cm.
ISBN	9783837928402 (paperback)
	9783837974447 (E-Book PDF)
LC classification	HQ76.3.G3 Q43 2018
Portion of title	Essays on racism, capitalism and sexual politics
Related names	Sweetapple, Christopher, editor.
	Bartal, Yossi, translator.
Subjects	Queer theory--Germany.
	Intersectionality (Sociology)--Germany.
	Racism--Germany.
	Capitalism--Germany.
	Sex role--Germany.
Notes	Includes bibliographical references.
Additional formats	9783837974447 PDF version
Series	Angewandte Sexualwissenschaft; volume 14

INDEX

A

access, 30, 72, 73, 78
acculturation, 4, 17, 18, 23, 25, 26, 53
action research, 111, 113
activism, 111, 113, 122, 126, 128
adaptation, 2, 15, 18, 19, 20, 51
additive approach, 61
adolescents, 24, 25, 49, 54
adults, 24, 50, 52, 67, 70, 75, 78
advancement, 79
affirmative action, 22
African American women, 25
African-American, viii, 2, 3, 4, 5, 6, 7, 9, 10, 11, 12, 13, 14, 15, 16, 17, 18, 19, 23, 25
alienation, 110, 112
American Psychological Association, 25, 26
analytical framework, 60
anthropology, 4, 87, 88
anxiety disorder, 49
Argentina, v, ix, 55, 56, 58, 61, 63, 64, 65, 69, 70, 72, 73, 76, 77, 78, 79
atmosphere, 5, 10
authenticity, 40, 115, 117

B

barriers, 14, 30, 95, 97
behaviors, 17, 51
benefits, 5, 17
bias, 5, 20, 46
biochemistry, vii
biological sciences, 19
bisexual, v, vii, viii, 27, 28, 29, 30, 31, 32, 33, 34, 35, 36, 37, 38, 39, 40, 41, 42, 43, 44, 45, 46, 47, 48, 49, 50, 51, 52, 53, 54
bivariate analysis, 62
Black students, 12, 13, 14, 15
black women, 106, 108, 121
brothers, 33, 71
Buenos Aires, 55, 63, 64, 65, 66, 67, 72, 73, 77, 78, 79

C

capitalism, 130, 131
case studies, ix, 55, 57
challenges, 3, 6, 10, 15, 20, 74, 77
child bearing, 32

childcare, 115, 117
childrearing, 115, 117
children, 14, 31, 32, 43, 53, 71, 104, 107, 115, 117
classes, 7, 12, 42, 91, 92
classification, 81, 82, 84, 85, 86, 88, 89, 90, 91, 92, 93, 94, 96, 99, 102, 103, 104, 107, 109, 110, 112, 114, 116, 118, 120, 121, 123, 125, 127, 130, 131
classroom, 95, 97, 101, 105, 108
climate, 84, 100
college campuses, 99, 100
college students, 5, 18, 22, 100
colleges, 20, 21, 22, 85, 86, 99
color, viii, 2, 10, 16, 18, 19, 21, 22, 25, 26, 48, 50, 51, 52, 101, 110, 112, 121, 122, 130
communities, 3, 4, 16, 17, 28, 30, 31, 32, 33, 38, 39, 40, 47, 53, 84, 125, 127, 128, 129
community, 3, 4, 5, 8, 15, 16, 17, 19, 29, 30, 31, 33, 35, 36, 38, 41, 45, 46, 47, 48, 52, 103, 122, 126, 128
complexity, ix, 46, 47, 55, 57, 72, 77
compositional diversity, 20
conception, viii, 55, 57, 124
conceptualization, 26
confidentiality, 34, 47
conflict, 4, 31, 33, 39, 45, 82, 83, 115, 117
conformity, 51
construction, 21, 87, 88, 130
conversations, viii, 2, 124, 125, 128
cooking, 14, 33
cultural domains, 3
cultural stereotypes, 72
culture, 4, 5, 11, 17, 19, 23, 24, 29, 30, 31, 32, 33, 37, 40, 43, 45, 46, 82, 83, 114, 116, 125, 128

D

dance, 42
dances, 42
danger, 58
database, ix, 22, 56, 62
deconstruction, ix, 55, 57
deficiencies, 10
deficit, 48
democracy, 111, 113
Denmark, 87, 88
dependent variable, 61, 62, 65
depression, 28, 51, 52
depressive symptoms, 51
depth, 46, 47, 114, 117
developmentalism, 90
disability, 59, 62, 79, 100, 105, 108
disclosure, 31
discrimination, 26, 29, 33, 37, 39, 41, 42, 45, 52, 79
diversity, 2, 6, 9, 10, 11, 16, 17, 20, 21, 22, 26, 48, 49, 51, 52, 99, 101, 105, 107
domain acculturation, 17, 18
domestic tasks, 72
domestic violence, 48

E

economic independence, 32
economic resources, 70, 71
economies of scale, 62
editors, 104, 107, 121
education, 4, 5, 6, 22, 26, 50, 67, 68, 84, 95, 96, 97, 98, 101, 104, 105, 106, 107, 109, 123
educational level, ix, 56, 58, 62, 64, 65, 67, 68, 69, 71
educators, 104, 105, 107, 108
elementary school, 63, 64, 65, 66, 68
empirical research, 57
employment, 60, 72, 115, 117

empowerment, 46, 59
energy, 19, 126, 128
environment, 3, 6, 10, 12, 15, 17, 18, 19, 39
epidemiology, 61
epistemology, 57, 122
equality, 90
equity, 79, 80, 104, 105, 106, 107, 108
ethnic, 3, 16, 17, 19, 21, 24, 25, 33, 34, 37, 45, 46, 48, 49, 51, 127, 129
ethnic identities, 3, 17
ethnicity, 16, 19, 24, 28, 29, 33, 37, 58, 62, 100, 104, 105, 106, 107, 109, 114, 116
experimental design, 60

F

families, 30, 31, 32, 38, 39, 40, 42, 45, 46, 47, 48, 49, 52, 53, 114, 116, 130
familism, 28, 31, 34, 38, 45, 54
family conflict, 114, 116
family functioning, 52
family life, 62, 71
family members, 31, 43, 45, 46, 71
feelings, vii, viii, 1, 10, 39, 40, 45
feminism, 33, 83, 84, 85, 86, 92, 119, 125, 128
fertility, 49
financial resources, 15
fluid, 18
focus groups, 110, 112
force, 40, 124
formation, 4, 16, 23, 115, 117
foundations, 46, 59
freedom, 33, 39, 103, 111, 113

G

gay men, 31, 50, 51, 52
gender, vii, viii, ix, 2, 14, 16, 17, 20, 21, 22, 25, 28, 29, 32, 33, 34, 37, 38, 39, 41, 45, 46, 48, 51, 52, 53, 55, 56, 58, 59, 60, 61, 62, 63, 64, 65, 66, 67, 68, 69, 70, 71, 72, 73, 74, 75, 76, 77, 79, 80, 81, 82, 83, 90, 91, 92, 93, 100, 104, 105, 106, 107,109, 114, 115, 116, 118, 119, 120, 125, 128
gender balance, 21
gender differences, 62, 68, 70, 71, 77
gender identity, 39
gender role, 32
Germany, 93, 130, 131
goal setting, 7
God, 31, 44, 98
graduate program, viii, 2, 3, 17, 18, 19
graduate school, 2, 3, 5, 7, 11, 12, 17, 20, 22, 23, 25
graduate students, 2, 6, 7, 22
group interactions, 8
grouping, 29, 32, 35, 47, 62

H

hair, 121
harassment, 41
harmony, 32, 45
HBCU, v, vii, 1, 2, 5, 6, 7, 8, 10, 11, 12, 14, 15, 16, 17, 19, 26
health, v, ix, 7, 28, 29, 47, 49, 51, 52, 53, 55, 56, 58, 59, 61, 62, 63, 64, 65, 67, 68, 69, 70, 71, 72, 73, 74, 75, 76, 77, 78, 79, 80, 90, 130
health care, 7, 78
health care system, 78
health services, 73, 76, 78
health status, ix, 56, 58, 62, 63, 65, 67, 68, 69, 70, 71, 72
high school, 7, 8, 13, 15, 68, 95, 97
higher education, 21, 22, 63, 67, 68, 69, 99, 100, 101
HIV, 29, 51
homeostasis, 32, 45
homes, 42
homosexuality, 51

household income, 62, 64, 65, 66, 67, 70
housing, ix, 56, 62
human, 4, 49, 72, 87, 88, 92, 111, 113
human capital, 49
human right, 111, 113
husband, 32
hypothesis, 60, 62

I

identity, viii, 2, 4, 6, 9, 12, 13, 15, 16, 18, 19, 21, 22, 23, 24, 25, 26, 28, 29, 30, 31, 32, 34, 36, 37, 39, 40, 42, 43, 45, 46, 47, 48, 50, 52, 53, 93, 94, 95, 96, 97, 98, 99, 100, 101, 102, 115, 117, 120, 122
identity politics, 21, 50, 102
imagination, 110, 111, 112, 113
income, ix, 56, 58, 62, 63, 64, 65, 66, 67, 69, 70, 71, 72, 75
incompatibility, 57
independent variable, 62, 63, 65, 67, 69
individuals, viii, 4, 17, 19, 27, 28, 29, 30, 31, 34, 36, 38, 53, 54, 59, 76
industries, 14
inequality, 57, 58, 59, 60, 72, 79, 80, 99, 129, 130
institutions, 2, 24, 93, 100
integration, viii, 28, 29, 30, 31, 37, 53, 111, 113
intentionality, 84
interactions, v, ix, 2, 6, 8, 18, 55, 56, 58, 59, 60, 62, 63, 65, 70, 74, 75
intersectional adaptation theory, 2, 15, 18, 19
intersectional identities, 4, 19, 95, 97
intersectional identity, viii, 2, 6
intersectional representation, 16
intersectionality, v, vii, viii, ix, 2, 17, 18, 20, 21, 25, 26, 27, 28, 29, 38, 47, 48, 49, 50, 55, 56, 57, 58, 59, 60, 61, 62, 69, 70, 72, 74, 75, 76, 77, 79, 80, 82, 83, 84, 85, 86, 87, 88, 89, 90, 91, 92, 93, 94, 95, 96, 98, 99, 101, 102, 103, 104, 105, 106, 107, 108, 109, 111, 113, 114, 116, 118, 119, 120, 121, 122, 123, 125, 127, 129, 130, 131
intervention, 52
isolation, vii, viii, 1, 2, 5, 15, 31
issues, 5, 9, 13, 22, 31, 47, 48, 52, 74, 102, 105, 108, 109

L

labor market, 72
labour market, 60
landscape, 125, 128
Latin America, 56, 77
Latinos, 48
Latinx, v, vii, viii, 27, 28, 29, 30, 31, 32, 33, 34, 35, 36, 37, 38, 39, 40, 41, 42, 43, 44, 45, 46, 47, 48, 105, 108
lead, 17
leadership, 84
learners, 105, 108
learning, viii, 2, 7
learning environment, viii, 2
leisure, 76
lens, vii, viii, 22, 25, 27, 28, 45, 114, 116
librarians, 122
lifetime, 30, 33
light, 9, 46
literacy, 120
logistic regression, ix, 55, 60, 61, 62, 63, 65, 67, 69, 70, 74
logistics, 82, 83
loneliness, 39, 40, 45, 47
love, 8, 48, 85, 86, 89, 95, 97

M

magnet, 8
majority, 11, 18, 39, 41, 45, 47, 62, 63

Index

management, 18, 24
marginalisation, 52
marketing, 126, 128
marriage, 30, 43, 46, 50
Maryland, 94, 96, 98
masculinity, 31, 51, 89
mass, 20, 119
mass media, 119
materials, 76
mathematics, 22, 23, 24, 25
matrix, 20, 115, 117, 129, 130
matter, 40, 57, 106, 108, 109, 111, 113
media, 36, 119, 124, 125, 127
mediation, 81, 82, 83
mentor, 5, 7, 9, 13, 14, 15
mentoring, 5, 7, 14
mentorship, 84, 100
metabolizing, 124
methodological strategies, 57
methodology, 57, 104, 107
Mexico, 73, 77
Miami, 130
middle class, 61
minorities, 7, 10, 11, 23, 24, 49, 52, 74
minority stress, vii, viii, 28, 29, 34, 37, 38, 44, 45, 46, 47, 48, 49, 51, 52
mobile communication, 82, 83
mobile phone, 81, 82, 83
mobile telephony, 81, 82, 83
models, ix, 4, 6, 12, 13, 14, 20, 26, 55, 56, 57, 61, 63, 65, 67, 70, 75
multiculturalism, 123
multiplicative, ix, 56, 58, 63, 70
multiplicative analysis, 63

N

narratives, 28, 34, 44, 45, 46, 47, 90
nationality, 100
negotiating, 4
networking, 7
neutral, 59
next generation, 23
nuclear family, 31

O

objectification, 49
odds ratio, 65, 68
one dimension, 29
opportunities, 10, 11, 13
oppression, 28, 29, 33, 46, 59, 94, 95, 96, 97, 100, 105, 107, 109, 111, 113
originality, 58
overlap, 120

P

parallel, 19
parenthood, 114, 116
parenting, 115, 117, 118
participants, viii, 6, 8, 28, 34, 35, 36, 37, 38, 39, 41, 42, 43, 45, 46, 53, 60, 115, 117
pedagogy, 94, 96, 105, 106, 108
peer relationship, 16
per capita income, 62
perceived health, ix, 56, 58, 62, 63, 64, 65, 67, 68, 69, 70, 71, 75, 77, 79
personal identity, 13, 19
persons with disabilities, 24
physical activity, 71, 76
physics, 22
platform, 126, 128
pleasure, 46
politics, 82, 83, 85, 86, 87, 88, 90, 102, 125, 127, 130, 131
population, ix, 3, 7, 19, 35, 55, 56, 58, 62, 63, 65, 69, 70, 71, 72, 76
population health, ix, 55, 58, 72
poverty, 123
power relations, 103, 104
prejudice, 29, 51

preservice teacher education, 105, 108
preservice teachers, 106, 108
president, 39
principles, 30, 46, 58, 59
procedural justice, 111, 112
professionalism, 122
professionals, 20, 101
programming, 7, 8
programming languages, 8
psychological distress, 31, 45
psychological well-being, 33
psychology, 21, 49, 77, 80
psychosocial factors, 72
public health, 58, 74, 79
punishment, 43

Q

qualitative research, 38
quality of life, 71, 76, 79
quantitative analysis, 61
quantitative research, 57, 74, 80

R

race, vii, viii, 2, 5, 13, 15, 16, 17, 19, 21, 22, 23, 24, 53, 58, 59, 60, 61, 62, 93, 94, 100, 104, 105, 106, 107, 109, 114, 115, 116, 118, 120, 123, 124, 125, 128, 129, 130
racism, 13, 32, 100, 105, 108, 130, 131
radio, 87, 88
reading, 85, 86, 102, 120
recommendations, viii, 2, 71
reconstruction, 5, 106, 108
recreational, 71
regression, ix, 56, 58, 59, 61, 62, 65, 67, 69
regression model, ix, 56, 59, 61, 70
rejection, 25, 29, 30, 37, 39, 53, 95, 97, 119
relationship quality, 50
relevance, 52

religion, 30, 31, 34, 37, 42, 43, 44, 45, 50, 53
religiosity, viii, 28, 30, 31, 36, 37, 38, 42, 43, 46
religious beliefs, 37
remediation, 5, 82, 83
renaissance, 126, 128
replication, 36
requirements, viii, 55, 57
researchers, 8, 18
resilience, 49, 52, 94, 96
resistance, 33, 87, 88, 106, 108, 118, 125, 127
resources, 15, 29, 30, 31, 62, 70, 71, 72
response, 111, 113
responsiveness, 87, 88
rights, iv, 77, 89, 93, 124
risk, 51
romantic relationship, 32
root, 62
rules, 44

S

safety, 115, 117
scholarship, 7, 104, 107, 124, 126, 128
school, 2, 3, 4, 5, 7, 8, 10, 11, 12, 13, 15, 17, 20, 22, 23, 25, 68, 71, 94, 95, 96, 97, 98, 104, 106, 107, 108, 110, 112, 123
schooling, 25, 95, 97, 110, 112
science, 5, 8, 14, 20, 23, 24, 25, 50, 51, 59, 74, 77, 89, 111, 113, 121, 122
secondary data, 61, 73
segregation, 5
self-discovery, 37, 39, 46
self-efficacy, 2, 16, 17
self-identity, 30, 122
self-perception, 62, 63, 67, 69, 70, 71, 72
semi-structured interviews, vii, viii, 1, 27
sex, 19, 35, 40, 43, 48, 51
sexism, 32

sexual identity, 31, 36, 37, 39, 40, 42, 48
sexual orientation, 30, 35, 39, 59, 80, 100
sexuality, 28, 32, 39, 40, 41, 42, 44, 45, 48, 59, 100
shortage, 71
social capital, 16, 21, 23
social change, 81, 82, 83
social class, 58, 59, 60, 70, 74, 100
social construct, 115, 117, 129, 130
social context, 8
social determinants of health, 59
social development, 16
social environment, 29
social exclusion, 52
social inequalities, 58, 61, 63, 69, 70, 72, 73
social inequities, 59
social justice, 38, 98, 103, 104, 105, 107, 109
social life, 87, 88
social network, 127, 129
social organization, 4
social phenomena, 124
social relations, 29, 81, 83
social relationships, 29, 81, 83
social stratification, 59
social stress, 52
social structure, 70
social support, 29, 30, 31, 45
social theory, 26, 102, 103, 104
socialization, 4, 22, 23, 53, 71
society, 12, 14, 15, 28, 46, 47, 80, 115, 117, 124, 125, 128
socioeconomic status, 100
sociology, 50, 74, 76, 99, 114, 116
software, 9, 37
spirituality, 31, 44, 50
statistical model, ix, 56, 57, 58, 59, 69, 70
statistics, 24
STEM, v, vii, viii, 1, 2, 3, 4, 5, 6, 7, 8, 9, 10, 13, 14, 15, 16, 17, 18, 19, 20, 21, 22, 23, 24, 25, 26, 101
STEM domain, 4

stereotypes, 12, 51, 95, 97, 106, 108
stereotyping, 13
stress, vii, viii, 17, 19, 28, 29, 34, 37, 38, 41, 44, 45, 46, 47, 48, 49, 51, 52, 71
stressors, 29, 45, 46
student populations, 3
substance abuse, 31, 52
substance use, 49, 51, 52
substance use disorders, 49, 52
suicide attempts, 28
syndrome, 24

T

teacher preparation, 105, 108
teacher relationships, 95, 97
teachers, 25, 94, 96, 104, 107
techniques, 9, 58, 61, 75
technology, 8, 23
tension, 11, 30, 33, 124
tensions, 124
tenure, 122
terrorism, 130
theoretical approach, 9
thoughts, 41
traditions, 47
transformation, 4
transition to adulthood, 91
transmission, 49

U

United States, vii, viii, 7, 49, 50, 51, 52, 55, 56, 85, 86, 94, 96, 97, 98, 101, 102, 122, 123, 127, 129, 130
universities, 2, 20, 21, 22, 26, 99, 101
unmasking, 122
urban, ix, 2, 6, 7, 49, 56, 62, 64, 65, 79

V

variables, ix, 49, 56, 58, 59, 62, 64, 65, 67, 68, 69
variations, 9
varieties, 20
vehicles, 16, 124
victimization, 33
victims, 33
violence, 21, 50, 53
vision, 89

W

war, 130
Washington, 18, 20, 24, 25, 26, 79
wealth, 109, 130
Wisconsin, 22
witchcraft, 123, 124, 125
workers, 32, 73, 90
workforce, 3
working class, 61, 110, 112

Related Nova Publications

PHOTOVOICE: PARTICIPATION AND EMPOWERMENT IN RESEARCH

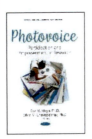

EDITORS: Eva M. Moya, PhD and Silvia María Chávez-Baray, PhD

SERIES: Social Issues, Justice and Status

BOOK DESCRIPTION: Photovoice: Participation and Empowerment in Research" describes Photovoice through the lenses of different communities and countries and discusses the methods and tools that make Photovoice appropriate for cross-cultural use.

HARDCOVER ISBN: 978-1-53616-201-1
RETAIL PRICE: $160

INTERNATIONAL PERSPECTIVES ON SOCIAL THEORY

EDITOR: Jake M. Seery

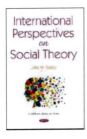

SERIES: Social Issues, Justice and Status

BOOK DESCRIPTION: International Perspectives on Social Theory opens with an identification of the characteristics that define contemporary social movements, including: a blurring and overlapping of taxonomical categories, an evolution towards a post-post-political stage, and a great variety and hybridization of organizational structures.

SOFTCOVER ISBN: 978-1-53615-991-2
RETAIL PRICE: $82

To see a complete list of Nova publications, please visit our website at www.novapublishers.com

Related Nova Publications

RACE AND ETHNICITY: INTERNATIONAL PERSPECTIVES, CHALLENGES AND ISSUES OF THE 21ST CENTURY

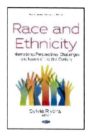

EDITOR: Sylvia Rivera

SERIES: Social Issues, Justice and Status

BOOK DESCRIPTION: *Race and Ethnicity: International Perspectives, Challenges and Issues of the 21st Century* first builds off the existing multicultural attachment literature to explore the concept of contextual and developmental adaptations of attachment bonds as it intersects with therapists' expectations for immigrant families living in the United States.

HARDCOVER ISBN: 978-1-53616-430-5
RETAIL PRICE: $230

EMOTIONS, TEMPORALITIES AND WORKING-CLASS IDENTITIES IN THE 21ST CENTURY

EDITORS: Michalis Christodoulou and Manos Spyridakis

SERIES: Social Issues, Justice and Status

BOOK DESCRIPTION: Given that Greece is the par excellence country of which the inhabitants went through the hardships of 2010 financial crisis, the authors of the volume are trying to explore the impact this crisis has upon the life-chances of working-class people.

HARDCOVER ISBN: 978-1-53616-203-5
RETAIL PRICE: $195

To see a complete list of Nova publications, please visit our website at www.novapublishers.com